THE BLACKRID

JULIA MARTIN

The
Blackridge House

A Memoir

Jonathan Ball Publishers
Johannesburg & Cape Town

Published in South Africa in 2019 by
JONATHAN BALL PUBLISHERS
A division of Media24 (Pty) Ltd
PO Box 33977
Jeppestown
2043

ISBN 978-1-86842-964-6
ebook ISBN 978-1-86842-965-3

Every effort has been made to trace the copyright holders and to obtain their permission for the use of copyright material. The publishers apologise for any errors or omissions and would be grateful to be notified of any corrections that should be incorporated in future editions of this book.

Twitter: www.twitter.com/JonathanBallPub
Facebook: www.facebook.com/JonathanBallPublishers
Blog: http://jonathanball.bookslive.co.za/

Cover by publicide
Design and typesetting by Nazli Jacobs
Printed and bound by CTP Printers, Cape Town
Set in Bembo

For her grandchildren
Sophie and Sky
and for Katie, Michelle, Zimisele, Lwazi, Sbulelo, and Kelsey,
who played in the garden

That thing we call a place is the intersection of many changing forces passing through, whirling around, mixing, dissolving, and exploding in a fixed location.

— *Rebecca Solnit*

To tell a story [...] is to relate, in narrative, the occurrences of the past, retracing a path through the world that others, recursively picking up the threads of past lives, can follow in the process of spinning out their own. But rather as in looping or knitting, the thread being spun now and the thread picked up from the past are both of the same yarn. There is no point at which the story ends and life begins.

— *Tim Ingold*

The vast wild
      the house, alone.
The little house in the wild,
      the wild in the house.
Both forgotten.

        No nature
    Both together, one big empty house.

— *Gary Snyder*

Contents

THE STORY

My mother, Elizabeth Madeline Martin, was born in 1918 and died in 2012. Her early childhood was spent at Blackridge, a semi-rural neighbourhood at the edge of Pietermaritzburg, in KwaZulu-Natal. In her final years, as recent memories dimmed, she felt increasingly unsettled, and experienced a powerful longing to return to that first home. By then, she was frail and bedridden, and had been living in Cape Town for decades. Though she remembered the place in detail, she had no idea of where exactly it was.

This is the story of a journey to find it, a story she was keen for me to tell. In writing it down, I have tried to be true to our many conversations, as well as to the kind people I met along the way, and to record accurately the contents of the domestic and public archives that the process opened up. But if the tale does ever wander into the country of imagination, I think she would have been glad. As she said to me one day, 'You can be as dramatic as you like when you're writing about this. My memory is full of blotches, like ink left about and knocked over.'

THE TREES

1.

'Well if you do find the place,' my mother said, 'I'd like you to bring me back two things: a photograph, and something growing from the garden.'

It was spring in Cape Town, and she was lying in the bed where she always lay, the metal cot sides up and a blue cushion strapped between the knees to prevent her legs from crossing and dislocating the hip.

'They run up and down,' she said, watching two grey squirrels through the sliding glass doors. 'Actually no, not up and down. They run up the long branch and then on to the next tree. Look at that one, just *rippling* along!'

Her room was upstairs, level with the tree. So the view from her bed was the life of its branches. This tree and all the others in the garden were the main reason she lived there, a nursing home chosen for its big trees, for the quality of light through morning leaves, for the joy of squirrels and birds, and for the fat koi swimming in the pond. All day they would drift in the dark water, bright torches of gold and red. If you dipped your hand in, they'd come up to the surface to hold your finger for a moment in their soft fish mouths, then dive back down into the deep.

Aside from such things, there was little to recommend about the facilities. Among various problems with the management, what particularly disturbed my mother was that they did not like pigeons. One afternoon she called me, crying, out of breath, furious, heartbroken, to say she'd been told she was no longer allowed to feed the birds that came to her verandah. Why? They make a mess.

I phoned the owner and explained that my mother, Elizabeth Martin, called the birds by name, and knew their characteristic ways and plumage. That at more than ninety years old, lying immobilised in this bed, most of the people she remembered were dead, the hours were so long, and the

7

world had become strange. But the ring doves, the turtle doves, and the rock pigeons returned each day and she could ask the nurses to feed them. When the owner remained unmoved, I said, Please try to imagine this is your own mother. Please understand. She has cared for others all her life and now she must submit to being washed and dressed, looked after in every detail. But she can still care for those birds, and she must. She is a mother. Then I mentioned St Francis (they are Catholics). I begged. The call was inconclusive, but the owner seemed to have softened a little. Afterwards I continued to buy birdseed, and the nurses, who were mostly kind, conspired to feed the doves and pigeons anyway.

On the particular day when I told my mother about the idea of visiting Blackridge, the birds had entirely occupied the verandah, and the room was filled with the violet smell of the tree she loved, the fragrance of syringa blossoms. From where I sat in the unused wheelchair beside her bed, the sweetness of those tiny stars was all the smell of a long warm afternoon in another garden. How I used to wish, in those days, that I could pick them, make posies for my dolls, even if they wilted so soon. But the delicate fragrance of syringa was mixed inextricably with the resonance of my paternal grandfather's warning.

'Every part of the tree is poisonous,' he would say, every time he visited. '*Every* part.'

Our syringas were the tallest trees in the garden, the canopy of those early years. But the smell of the flowers is infused, even now, with my grandad's words. He had studied botany and loved trees, and so complete was his conviction that I never wondered to find out whether he was right. For he was a man accustomed to authority, and I was a girl then, wary of transgression.

These days the tree evokes a different prohibition. Like black wattle, lantana and bugweed, the syringa tree, *Melia azedarach,* is listed in some regions of South Africa as a Category 1 declared weed, a tree that must, by law, be removed and destroyed immediately, an alien invader, foreign, dangerous, undesirable.[1]

'What a stupid idea,' my mother said, laughing, when I told her. And then, more seriously, 'I would be so upset if they chopped it down.'

'Nobody is going to hurt your tree, don't worry. But syringas actually *are* a problem, especially along the rivers.'

I told her how colonials brought the trees from the East as ornamentals, transporting them to wherever in the world they would grow. These days it's birds that spread the golden berries, and in some parts of the country the edges of rivers are choked more with syringas than with any other alien plant species. The trees displace the indigenous vegetation, drink up the run-off, and can even dam the flow altogether. So people who are serious about water do say syringas should be eradicated.

But my mother had little interest in such arguments, or in the idea that grey squirrels were also alien invaders, or that pigeons were vermin, flying rats. Strapped all day to the blue cushion in the nursing home bed, her mind absorbed the undulating line of the long syringa branch that reached towards her verandah, the lichens that grew on its bark, the beings that passed through. She knew the bunches of flowers that bloom and fall, the little berries, the pattern of twigs and leaves against the sky, the movement of the tree when it rocked in the wind. When the pigeons came, she loved to watch their jostle and strut. How the one she named Solomon would be tender to his wife but fight all the others to secure his rights to the grain. How deferent the ring doves and cinnamon doves were to the pigeons. And who had a sore foot, the toes constricted by tangled thread.

Beyond the immediate particulars of pigeons, squirrels, and this long branch, my mother had forgotten the rambling garden she cultivated when I was a girl, watering and tending in the early mornings as I watched her from my bedroom window, a tall figure in a long white dressing gown in the early light, under the syringas. She had forgotten the oak sapling my father planted and the tree that it became. She had forgotten his flagrant bougainvillea hedge, and his roses and intermittent vegetables. She had forgotten my father. Most of the time she would forget that she'd ever had a daughter.

Now, when the lifetime of stories that made up a self had almost disappeared, what she had left was early childhood and the present moment. As other things faded into forgetting, what remained were a small wood-

and-iron house, and a garden with deep trees. And water, there had to be water. In the gathering dark of the nursing home bed, that first place gleamed like a lighted window.

'At Blackridge,' she said, 'for some reason the baby bats used to get right down into the curled-up banana leaves. If you touched the leaf, you would feel the little thing moving inside.'

Across the years, the touch of small fingers reaches to me now: even now, the feel of a baby bat asleep in a curled leaf.

2.

For a while the phone calls had been getting more insistent. She might be angry ('I can't stay here another second, please come and fetch me home') or matter of fact ('Hello darling, I've had lunch and I'm ready to go now') or vaguely confused ('Where are you? I need to come home') or simply desperate ('I've just arrived here and this place is unspeakable. Please let me come back'). At such times, even the comfort of the tree with its pigeons and squirrels could not reach her.

At first my mother would call during the day, sometimes several times. Then the midnight calls began, wrenching me from sleep to run down-stairs and talk, and afterwards return to lie for hours with a pounding heart.

Usually I would say something like, 'Everything's all right. Look around the room. You can see your pictures, your books . . . That's where you live now, you've been there several years.'

But the indefinite article that makes all the difference between home and a home sapped my conviction. For she knew, and I knew, that home was never like this. They never played this sort of music at home. They never ate this sort of food. Meals were not eaten alone with an aluminium spoon, or carried in on a tray by a person who speaks to one in that special intonation that is reserved for babies, pets, and people to whom we wish to condescend. And the smells of the place, the smell of old people, sick people, cleaning fluids, these smells are different from the smell of home. And the pills, all the unknown pills to be swallowed each day. It was never like this at home. It was never like this.

Anyone could find the institutional culture of a nursing home distress-ing, particularly at the end of a life when the slow diminishing route from family house to cottage to retirement flat has brought you at last to this one room, this single bed, the last stop on the line. But the terror of exile is especially acute when you wake up each morning and you don't know where you are, or what happened yesterday, and there is nothing familiar in the room, and the people who greet you are all foreigners.

'These people get on my nerves,' she said one day. 'There's no friendliness at all. Of course, the trees here are lovely. Never seen such green . . . It's like walking into a puddle and getting splashed.'

'What is?'

'Not being able to remember. Because your brain gets muddled and mixes things up. It's a great sadness.'

In the various strange states of confusion and memory loss that doctors call the dementias, the longing for home recurs as something persistent and unrequited. Even when a person is living in a house she has known all her life, the disease of forgetting may render it alien, unrecognisable. She wants to go home. To be the person she was when she lived at home. Perhaps in the silence of her memory she detects the echo of a time when things and people resided in their places, and she was present to herself. At home. She felt at home. Please make yourself at home. Please take me back home. Please.

The way she put it when I picked up the phone one particular afternoon was, 'I can't stand this atmosphere. I don't have any friends.' And then, 'I'm homesick. I want to go home. I've been living a strange life for the last few years, away from Natal.'

I tried to explain that it was nearly thirty years since she had left KwaZulu-Natal, but she did not believe it. I said her old home was no longer there, and she did not believe that either. I said I had thought about the possibility hundreds of times, but that Michael and the twins and I just could not have her come and stay with us at our house, that we were all working or at school, and she needed more care than we could provide.

'But nobody does anything for me here!' she said, astonished and affronted at the idea that she might need looking after.

'Yes they do.' I was arguing again, pointless. 'You can't walk any more.'

'Of course I can walk.'

'And the wheelchair in your room?'

'That's for *long* walks. But otherwise I just walk around a lot.'

12

'And your meals. They bring you your meals.'

'They do not! I have my meals in the dining room. I had breakfast and lunch there, and I'll have my supper there too. I can't *remember* when I last had a meal in bed!'

'Lunch.'

'Oh no. I wonder where you got that idea from.'

In that moment, the mind's determination to escape, to find its way home, made it possible for her to construct whatever was needed to fit that fierce imperative.

For other residents of the nursing home who were not bedridden, there was in fact a small chance, even with all the gates and cameras in place, of making the break. So far, it had happened once since she had been there when a woman called Goldie walked out of the gate one morning with her shopping basket and never returned. I met her a few weeks later, on a city street. She was looking a little disreputable, but pleased and defiant.

'I'll never go back,' she told me. 'It's a terrible place.'

The others were all still there. The old, the sick, the dying, the man who used to insist he was my mother's husband, the woman who played air guitar in the corridor and sang romantic songs in Portuguese, the woman who had recently begun to hit the nurses in the face, the young man with no legs, the ones who simply sat and stared. And among this gathering of the lost was my mother herself in her upstairs room, not mixing with the other residents, choosing, at the cost of loneliness, to retain a measure of psychic space that was still her own.

It seemed easier to respond to Goldie's dramatic and competent escape than to my mother's intense feeling of displacement. The literature on dementia care is full of practical suggestions on what to do about wanderers, people who want to go home. But there was nothing to help me answer this longing that occupied the heart like the chafe of a bedsore that would not heal.

'I just don't know what to say.'

'Well, I understand the answer's no. About coming home.'

'It's very hard for me to say this . . .' I began.

She was thinking I was her mother, her sister, anything but her daughter. And all she wanted was for me to take her home. I felt it then, the weariness of it all. And the terror, hers and now mine, of waking to a place where there is nobody to hold you.

'It sounds as though I'm rejecting you,' I went on. 'But I'm not. Please trust me when I tell you that we just don't have what it takes to care for you. You're ninety-two years old. It's normal to need looking after.'

'Ninety-two? That's why I'm homesick.'

It was after this anguished conversation, or one of many like it, that I began to form the idea of visiting KwaZulu-Natal and looking for her family house at Blackridge, the only home she could remember.

It was not clear why I wanted to do this. Perhaps I felt that, if my mother could not go herself, then somehow I could find the place for her. Or perhaps I was hoping that, in some inexplicable way, I might meet her there. She liked the idea when I mentioned it, but could give me no hint of an address.

'My memory is . . . gone, you know,' she said.

Then she began telling stories about a garden with mangoes and a stream in it, a small house full of dogs and children, a wild hill growing with flowers and grasses.

From the nursing home room where she lay, you could see the syringa tree. Inside, the walls were filled with images of people, trees, houses, animals, and flowers which the nurses had drawn. She would give them crayons, coloured pencils, and paper whenever they wanted them, and it got them drawing, many for the first time in their life. One of them told me, 'We can breathe in here.'

Now she had given me a task too: to bring back a photograph and something growing, if I ever found the house. All I had intended was a short journey to another province. But the force of my mother's imagination made me feel like one who must cross over into a distant realm, make it through the mists and the mud of forgotten things, pass through dark forests, and return with something salvaged from the dead, and something living.

I must do this before it was too late. I still had no directions.

3.

On weekends I would bring birdseed for the pigeons, rusks for my mother to eat during the week when the nursing home food became intolerable, and biscuits to share with her grandchildren, Sophie and Sky.

'Tell me about Blackridge,' I said in the first of many conversations.

She hesitated.

'It makes me cry.'

Then, 'Okay, the things I remember: Cyril Green. They lived in a house below ours, across the road, and we both had elder brothers and sisters. So we played together. We played trains for him, and family for me. In *our* garden. His people didn't welcome people playing. But our house was very friendly. Lovely trees all around. A stream at the bottom of the garden. A railway above and the road below. It wasn't a proper river, but we called it a river. It needed a bridge over it, big enough to have railings at the side.'

Cyril. Family. Trees. Railway. Stream. Each was a primal feature of her world, but the railway line and the stream were defining elements. The railway would not be difficult to locate, but if I wanted to find my mother's house, there had to be a stream.

'Now Cyril and I used to play all the time,' she went on, 'and he brought me back secrets from school because he went to school before me. He told me a secret. He showed me his *banana*. It was very secret. He said, "Look, this is what is called a *banana*."'

The twins, twelve years old, were amused. We all laughed.

'Oh we used to play,' she said, smiling. 'He used to pretend to drive, to be the engine of the train, and I used to come along behind carrying all the luggage. We used to watch the trains go by. The train driver was a friend of ours and he used to throw an apple to us.'

15

We. Together. Secrets. Playing. In the album I found a picture of Betty, as her family called her, and Cyril. They are standing together in the garden, a little awkward before the camera, but smiling mischievously, each holding the hand of one of her dolls. The garden is a realm of barefoot summer, a world where you can play.

The other picture of her from this time must have been taken on the same day, in almost the same place. Her hair is untidy, long. Her arms and legs are bare, and she is wearing a loose cotton dress, a little bracelet. Flopped in a chair on the grass, she is a small mother facing the camera with her assembled children. One doll is on her lap, while another doll sits in a little bed, and one in a chair, wooden furniture made by her father. Behind is a stand of tall gum trees, a hedge along the back near a small corrugated iron structure and, to the left of Betty, the edge of a wood-and-iron house.

It was a warm day in the garden at Blackridge in 1925. Someone had a camera, and hoped by that device to wrest some tangible thing from the flow of change and forgetting: a six-year-old girl whose smile is so wide that it creases her eyes and wrinkles her nose, or the tenderness of bare feet, crossed at the ankle.

The third picture of Betty as a little girl was so tiny that, once my mother had identified the dog sitting at her feet as Bindle, I almost disregarded it. Only some time after her death, when the image was scanned and digitally enlarged, did I really see it for the first time: a picture that both recalls and resists a whole genre of Victorian and Edwardian pictures of little girls posed for the camera. She looks about four years old, and someone has dressed her in a pretty white dress for the occasion, brushed her curly hair, and tied a ribbon over her head for an Alice band. But where the studio photographer might have put an oversized bunch of roses or lilies in her arms and seated her on a small throne amid some pastoral fantasy, the branch she is holding has been picked from the garden, and her seat is one of the family's wicker chairs, placed in the morning sun beside what looks like an avocado tree in a realm of ferns and weeds and unkempt grasses. Blackridge. At her feet, bare feet that don't yet touch the ground, Bindle faces the camera with interest.

Discovering the picture again after her death, it was her small bare feet that touched me most. And the strength of the expression on her face. Instantly recognisable.

'What about your other friends?' Sophie asked.

'Well there was Charmian. Charmian Turton, with her *long* beautiful blond ringlets. I think her mother had died and her grandmother was bringing her up. She came to visit in a white dress, and she wasn't allowed to get dirty. She had a *beautiful* expensive doll that nobody was allowed to touch. Now what was the good of a doll like that? She would be brought down to the house by her nanny. I think Cyril and I would go and climb up the mango tree to escape from her. We used to crawl along the branches.'

The mango tree had been part of the story of her childhood for as long as I could remember. It was tall, with dense glossy leaves to hide among, good branches for climbing, fragrant sprays of little flowers, and the fruit, the fabulous, sticky fruit.

Its ancestors came from India, where people have been cultivating them for thousands of years. The fleshy orange fruit would be eaten raw, preserved, or cooked, turned into medicines or used in religious ceremonies, the patterns of the flowers embroidered into paisley shawls, or the tree woven into magical songs and the stories of gods. At first, the spread of seeds happened gradually as passing monks and traders packed mangoes into their luggage. Then, things became more systematic. When mangoes arrived at Kew Gardens in the early nineteenth century, they were found to be so delicious that soon they were being shipped from that fabulous garden metropolis to satellite botanical gardens around the world. Within a few years, under Queen Victoria's administrators, the plant was classified among the Flora of British India.[2]

The tree in my mother's garden would have been a specimen of the plant they named the common mango, *Mangifera indica*, its new name a record of inscription in the taxonomies of a science whose tracks had already criss-crossed the planet. Mangoes were more useful as a commodity than the poisonous syringa. But they were a less profitable crop than the sugar or tobacco or certain other plants among the multitude of species whose seeds, cuttings, or root stock were, in the space of a couple of centuries, being transported over long distances and transplanted into unfamiliar soils, changing forever the ecologies of the places where they began to grow.

Would it be heavy-handed to say that Betty and Cyril, and all the other children with an exotic mango tree in the garden, were ingesting the fruits of conquest and imperial trade? In one sense the common mango at Blackridge was indeed another node in the global grid of Empire, its tropical produce a thing of power and information. But for my mother the tree was particular and alive. The ramifying branches were a leafy place for hiding with your best friend, and the delicious, hairy, juicy flesh of the mango tasted so sweet. How perfect that messy mango was then, fibres caught in the teeth, your face and hands and dress all wet with sticky juice, young skin tasting of summer.

'Gorgeous. Mangoes,' my mother said, looking back into that tree from the nursing home bed. 'And bananas and apples from the garden. Those things were just taken for granted. I remember boiled mealies too.'

Then she told us about Roy Johnstone, the only other boy she knew apart from Cyril, and how they tried to escape from him as well as Charmian by climbing the tree.

'When he came to play, Cyril and I would go and scuttle up the mango tree,' she said. 'So my mother would call us, "Come on, come out and play with Roy." And Roy would look proud.'

She grinned.

'One time we prayed. I knew about praying because I had been to Sunday school. I didn't go back because I thought the people were rude. They talked about Abraham's bosom and I said I'm never going back there. My mother was glad. It was a nuisance to take me there, all the way up to the little church near the station. And Sunday school was boring. I remember that when I said I wasn't going back, Letty and Doodie and Jock and Barts and Mother all said, "Thank goodness!"'

Betty was the fifth of six children. She was often a nuisance, she told us, to Mother and her elder siblings, and having to be walked up to church was just another instance. But if Abraham's bosom was an excuse to get out of Sunday school, it also worked as a successful appeal to the family's

Edwardian silence about the body. Whatever might have taken place in private in the bedrooms of the house, bodies were unmentionable. She knew, without being told, that Cyril's banana was a secret.

How compelling, then, that transgressive word, remembered across all these years.

'It was very rude to say bosom,' she said. 'But to picture Abraham, a man, with a bosom! You tried not to think about it at night.'

'Anyway,' she continued, 'I knew you had to kneel down. So Cyril and I both knelt down on the lawn with the dolls and the teddy bears and prayed: "Please God, send Roy the toothache." I don't remember whether it worked. I suppose it didn't. He was lonely. He didn't have anyone to play with.'

4.

I called the Office of the Surveyor General in Pietermaritzburg and was put through to a person called Mr Marais.

From what my mother had said I now knew that the house must have been situated quite a way from the little church, that you had to walk 'up' to get there, that the railway line was above the house and a road below it, that in the garden there was a great mango tree and a stream. Or perhaps it was all rather different from this. The family left Blackridge in 1926 when she was eight, so whatever she could tell me were the memories of a small child, traces recollected more than eighty years later across a smudgy realm of forgetting.

Then I found a faded sepia image stacked among a heap of old photographs in the nursing home cupboard. It was a small wood-and-iron house. My mother identified it. Blackridge.

'Yes,' said the voice on the other end of the phone, 'that's the old station, the old railway line. It's close to Sweetwaters Road. There's an old church there. We call it the paper church because it's made of that cardboard with some sort of tar over it. There's a boarding establishment around there, and then three or four old houses to the right. No, I don't think any of the old houses have been pulled down.'

I mentioned the stream.

'Yes, there's one that could have a stream. You take a left into Uplands Road, or Albany Road. Or is it Simpson Road? Ask your mother if she remembers any of the road names. At the railway station there's a narrow bridge. Ask her if she remembers the bridge.'

'You seem to know the area so well. You're being so helpful.'

'Well I walk there sometimes.'

Mr Marais explained how busy he was, how many requests he was dealing with.

Then he said, 'But email me the photo. Maybe I can go and have a look for it on one of my walks.'

It wasn't a response I could have anticipated when I called. I'd not expected to find someone at the surveyor general's who knew a place by walking.

Instead, I'd imagined the phone ringing in an airless set of offices lined with racks of old cadastral maps and bulging files, the computers full of diagrams and boundaries. If not quite surveillance, the idea evoked a sort of quintessential state headquarters of measurement and cartography: that single view from above that comprehends a living neighbourhood in terms of ownership and parcels of land, plots its precise location from a series of points, and can admit neither people nor stories. It was what I thought I was looking for just then. Co-ordinates.

Before we said goodbye, he told me his name. Francois.

5.

A quest is never what you expect it to be.

A few days later, I met a librarian called Andrew who offered to help me trace the house. Then an email appeared from him that reminded me of a narrative I would have preferred not to inherit.

Our communication began with my mother saying that her father taught at the Pietermaritzburg Technical College during the Blackridge years. This gave me the idea that that institution might just have a record of his address at the time. So I called the library of the current Durban University of Technology, where I was put through to the friendly young voice of a man who identified himself as Andrew Naicker. I told him what I was looking for, and a couple of days later he emailed to say he had done some sleuthing.

The old Tech where my grandfather worked had later become the Umgungundlovu FET College (Msunduzi Campus). But as for archival material from the 1920s, Andrew wrote, 'Apparently much of the stuff dating back to that period has been either lost or discarded during the merger process that the college underwent. Go figure.'

The next day, he told me, 'I happen to have a cousin who works for the PMB municipality. I am hoping that he could use his resources to find the address you seek (fingers crossed). Will get on the horn now and let's see what my cousin comes up with. Keep you posted.'

The day after that, there was nothing from the cousin, but Andrew had now found a different lead.

'I managed to get this invaluable information about your grandpa,' he wrote. 'It seems that Mr Smallie had quite an illustrious military career.'

The email went on to outline my grandfather's activities in a volunteer regiment, the Natal Carbineers, around the turn of the century. Andrew

23

listed the dates on which he was promoted (Corporal, Lieutenant, Captain, Brevet Major, Major), the various 'operations' in which he was more significantly involved, the details of his mention in Lord Kitchener's dispatches for marked good work near Nondweni, Zululand, 28 July 1901, and a list of medals and clasps. It emerged that Alan Watson Smallie not only fought from beginning to end in what he called the Boer War, but was also a senior officer in the forces enlisted to quell the Zulu rebellion of 1906.

What was I to do with the information? Warfare was repugnant, and dusty stories of imperial conquest and occupation were unlikely to help me find the place. But after Andrew's email I could no longer ignore the old suitcase at the top of my mother's cupboard in the nursing home. Though I had never paid it much attention, it had always been around in a back room somewhere, a collection of her father's papers. It was not what I was looking for, but on the next visit I took it down anyway, brought it home.

When I opened the suitcase it looked like an archive.

Someone had long since removed the ceremonial red coat with its brass buttons, but the main documents were still there. The oldest manuscript, Alan Smallie's *Diary of the Trip of the Natal Volunteers to England for the Festivities at the Diamond Jubilee, 1897,* had been re-bound in red leather by my mother, and looked quite recent. Another notebook, large and cloth-covered, had been eaten by rats or mice all around the edges so that the marks of their little teeth made its brown pages seem more ancient than they really were, like someone's idea of a parchment map. It was the first of two books in which he had copied out the letters he'd written to his parents during the South African War. The second volume of letters was a blue-and-brown marble-covered notebook, its paper a little better preserved. Then there was a heap of uncollected fragments (photographs, certificates, newspaper cuttings, a sort of narrative curriculum vitae) and another collection of letters assembled in a sheaf of plastic sleeves.

My grandfather died long before I was born, but the suitcase archive evoked at once a person who wanted very much to remember and to be remembered. To have been there. To have been someone. Though he had no formal education after school, his commitment to the practice of writing suggested that his trust in storytelling, in the power of inscription and of orderly syntax, must have been a defining feature of who he was.

During his war, the one that made a man of him and irrevocably shaped the country that became South Africa, young Alan Smallie wrote letters home every few days. His mother Flora Mary, the first of us women to safeguard his project, kept each one. Much later, near the end of his life once six tall children were grown, he spent the evenings transcribing what amounted in the end to 435 foolscap pages of the War letters, and writing a preface to the collection that included a modest account of his part in the campaign. The correspondence was never published, but after he died, my mother took care of the whole assemblage. Now that she had quite forgotten it, the suitcase seemed to have passed on to me. Posterity.

On every page I turned, my ancestor had left an easy flowing inky trail of well-formed words and sentences, stories that set out to tell the truth (or, if not truth, then simply stories, the ones he wanted remembered) in all the certainty of a fine Victorian hand. But the old paper was brittle, a fragile legacy, and his words crumbled apart at the least thoughtless touch.

The suitcase had appeared in my path like an old hag's gift pressed into the traveller's hands along some mythic roadside. Such gifts are inexplicable, but you cannot ignore them. I set out to read everything I could before we left for Blackridge.

6.

Alan Smallie was just twenty-one, a fine upstanding fellow with direct blue eyes and a neat moustache, when he was chosen to travel to England with a small regiment of Natal Volunteers for the celebration of Queen Victoria's Diamond Jubilee. The occasion, which extended over several weeks in mid-1897, was a public relations exercise of extraordinary proportions, a vast transnational spectacle whose compelling imagery was to seal a story of monarchy and empire that would last the rest of his life.

They set off, he says, with the colonel's reminder to do their best for the colony, and to remember that they had the credit of Natal on their shoulders.[3] His daily journal records a dutiful young man's cheerful insertion into the imperial discipline of uniforms, marches, and parades, and the minute details of authority and promotion.

At the centre of it all was the tale of Britannia and her diamond queen: Empress of India, great white mother of her people at home and in the colonies, to whom all ranks were drawn from regions far across the globe. Like ants they came, like bees swarming to greet her at the epicentre of the world where the colonial forces were treated to all the concerts, plays, dinners, tailored clothes, flag-waving crowds, sweaty processions, and ceremonial pomp that London could provide, including a great display of successive waves of some of the industrialising Empire's more exotic subjects – Maoris, Malays, Sikhs, Jamaicans, and Chinese.

Of his own feelings, my grandfather records very little, but he writes that nearly every day the soldiers marched and paraded in strict formation. On the occasion of the main procession when, as others have estimated, two million people came to the city (crowding the windows of all the buildings, and the roofs, he says, cheering the colonials most heartily, singing 'Rule Britannia,' and 'God Save the Queen' and 'Auld Lang Syne', and giving the Volunteers once they had halted at St Paul's as much champagne as they could drink), he writes that, though it was a magnificent show, the soldiers themselves could not see much of the spectacle and did not see royalty.

But ten days later, sitting upright on his borrowed horse on one particular morning, young Smallie was granted a glimpse of the person in a carriage on whom it all converged: the flags, the people, the goods, the guns, the shipping lines that transported them across the waves, the global routes of conquest, industry, and trade, the lines of brutal force that held them all subject.

On this, the forty-eighth day, he records in his diary that Her Majesty asked questions about the different uniforms, and that (having come to a halt immediately in front of the royal carriage), he distinctly heard Her Majesty's voice.

How exciting it must have been for him to be present in that gathering, to have been an utterance, a word, even a syllable, in the compelling story of the sovereign queen and her dominions. How eagerly they must have believed, colonial soldiers like my young grandfather dispersing afterwards from the great metropolis to the far provincial towns from

27

whence they came, believed or wanted to believe, that its civilising imprint was benevolent.

Yet if the bright gloss of an Empire built on war and plunder and deceit seemed – at least during those brief weeks of Jubilee – quite dazzling, in subsequent years the dark shadow of this spectacle would become more difficult to ignore. In one man's lifetime, my grandfather's, a series of public actions would manifest the terrible cost of all that glory. The suitcase archive documents a long imperial war followed soon after by a massacre. Once that was done, and the ground rules for racist power secured, he saw the business of supremacy turn to repeated assaults on the environment – the industries of timber, sugar, monoculture – and he took part in the chemical warfare required to sustain its subjugation. Was my ancestor complicit? Of course. Now even the wild hill at Black-ridge where he loved to walk is occupied by plantations and the net of global trade.

But this was all yet to come. In 1897 he was young and full of anthems and parades.

Even so, it is possible – I like to think – to discern at times in his Jubilee diary the strain of some less congruous sounds that gave a hint of other voices. During the steamship crossing to England he notes the presence of a character whose curious dirge was to make its way through the family's transmission of songs over more than a hundred years.

Without comment he writes, 'The following is the "grace" that we all sing, standing, before each meal: "The birds of the air fell a-sighing and a-sobbing, When they heard of the death of poor Cock Robin, When they heard of the death of poor Cock Robin. All's well."'

I remembered it then as one of the songs my mother had sung when I was little.

'Oh yes,' she said when I asked, old face creased in a smile. 'And you know Barts, my eldest brother, he used to sing it to me too. It was when I stopped going to Sunday school.'

Despite God, King, and Country, Alan Smallie never really got formal religion, and at six his youngest daughter had also given up orthodox piety.

'So instead of church, you used to go for walks with Barts?' I said.

'That's very, very vivid.'

Remembering, she raised herself from the pillows. How thin her arms had become, and her hair, two thin grey plaits.

'At Blackridge, he would take me every Sunday on a walk,' she said. 'One walk we did often was to the top of the hill on the other side of the railway line. We would sit and look. And he would open up his lunch, and share it with me. Sometimes there was even a small bar of chocolate. And then he would sing. Sing and sing: "Cock Robin. Who killed Cock Robin?"

'I think that's where I first got my feeling for live creatures,' she continued. 'Those walks. He didn't lecture me about them, but they were sort of all part of it. I can hear him now.'

She started to sing then in a low, wavering voice, 'All the birds of the air fell a-sighing and a-sobbing, When they heard of the death of poor Cock Robin . . .'

It's an old song, wonderfully mournful and strange. Once the Sparrow has confessed to killing Cock Robin with his bow and arrow, each of the other creatures – the Fly, the Fish, the Beetle, the Bull and all the birds – takes a turn to speak, offering to make his shroud, to dig his grave and to assume the roles of parson, pall-bearer, psalm-singer, and so on that are required to perform the last rites.

From high up on the Ridge with her brother on a Sunday morning, they might have glimpsed the little church down near the railway line. But the hill was fragrant with grasses and many flowers, the world humming with bees and beetles, a universe of tiny creatures at your feet, the sky alive with birds. High in the Mistbelt grassland, that ancient ecology beloved of buck and cattle and human beings, the world was vast and young and very, very old, and the local site of the Anglican Church must have seemed a smaller thing than it was to those inside the building. High on the wide, wild hill at Blackridge, knee-deep in the grass, Sundays were for walking together, sitting together, your brother singing. And each time the curious story of Cock Robin and his sentient community of birds and animals accompanied them, like their father's grace on the ship to England.

More than eighty years later, on the particular visit to my mother at the nursing home when she remembered it, the joy of Barts's melancholy song seemed as clear as ever. At other times her father, her favourite, seventy years dead, was with her too.

'You felt so good, walking with Dad,' she would say, legs strapped to the cushion, body confined to the bed. 'You knew that everything was all right, just walking and wandering through the long green grass with him. I can feel it now, walking with my father. That lovely grass, just walking together . . .'

7.

The path to home tends to meander. It is obscure. Or perhaps it is a road that is broken and lost, an old track irretrievably washed away. Perhaps home, when you find it, has been erased, the big trees cut down for townhouses. Or perhaps it is still there, but small and mean, a shameful thing you would rather not have found. As I prepared to visit Blackridge, the fears began to take form. Could I bear to arrive and find my mother's home – grove of memory, green of childhood – destroyed? Did I really have to test my courage against the real? Perhaps the truth of it after all was that there is no path: simply the play of a small child long ago in a world that seemed familiar, simply the stories of a forgetful old woman.

The wood-and-iron structure in the photograph looked smaller than I had imagined it, yet the place was large enough to house the growing mind of a child. And over the years it became an assemblage of the past. By the time she was telling stories about Blackridge in the nursing home, it had become inhabited by events and people from many years hence – like the garden in a hermetic *Ars Memoriae*, which she'd populated with images compelling enough to guide her through memory when she returned to walk its paths.

So when Sky showed her a recent collection of family photographs that spanned four generations, she told us they were all taken at Blackridge.

Another time she said, 'I used to draw pigs a lot because you could do them easily and get the right expression.'

She was lying with Sophie beside her on the bed, paging together through a sketch book dated 1938, ten years after the family had left the neighbourhood.

'Did you draw as a child?' Sophie asked.

'I don't know. I made mud pies. That I know.'

'When did you draw the pigs?'

'At Blackridge.'

'And when did you make mud pies?'

'With Cyril. Roy didn't. He used to destroy them.'

I began reading what I could about memory and forgetting, hoping for further images that would speak to our experience. One neurology text described the brain's system of many billions of neurons as a switchboard, or a network, and compared its memory capacity to massive libraries. Other writers imagined it as a vast forest, an image I liked because of the way it resonated with her love of wildness.

And, of course, neurons do look like microscopic trees. I learnt that the dendrites (the word derives from the Greek *déndron*, 'tree'), extend like ramifying branches from the cell body of the neuron, while the long filament of the axon projects like the trunk of the tree. When our brain is healthy, the flow of thoughts, desires, fears, longings, stories, and all the impulses that enable us to live and move and breathe, travel along a myriad such pathways in communication with one another. An electrical signal moves down the trunk of the axon until it reaches the synapses at the roots of the neuron. There, as it makes the leap across to the synaptic terminals in the dendrites of another neuron, it momentarily transforms to a chemical flow. And then again, in the marvellous flickering light show of the brain, it becomes electricity once more, travelling down the axon, and on to the next neuron.

In this lively mesh of mind, kelp forests ripple in the underwater tide. A myriad roots grow and ramify underground. All the rivers in the world are streaming to the sea. And there are trees, uncountable trees, a whispering jungle in the head.

When I asked my mother what it was about Blackridge that made it so special, her answer pointed not to the place itself, or the people, but to the quality of the child's awareness. It was a quality of freshness that her life as a creative person had been finely tuned to recognise.

She said, 'I heard someone say once that the first six to seven years of your life are very vivid.'

'It's a bit like you've got an old koki pen,' Sky said, 'and you're writing with it. The first bit of your writing is very clear. Then it becomes more faint.'

Memories might be texts stored in a virtual library, pages assembled in an archive, words written with a child's koki pen that are more or less distinct. But I came to see them also, more literally, as well-worn paths in the wild. In this sense they are not so much things but processes. For it is the act of remembering, and of remembering again, that creates and retains a memory. So the practitioner of the *Ars Memoriae* recalls the so-called objects of memory by imaginatively visiting again the location where they reside: walking the paths of that place in the mind. In a similar way, the memories of Blackridge are well-trodden neural pathways, first walked as a child and subsequently confirmed and strengthened over a lifetime's repetition.[4]

My mother's doctors said it was unlikely that she had Alzheimer's disease. But whatever they called it, her state of mind seemed to be one of those conditions in which the lively communicative systems of the brain progressively break down, and the brain literally shrinks. My readings explained that, if you are suffering from a dementia such as Alzheimer's, one of the earliest regions of your brain to be affected is the hippocampus. This is a region that processes short-term memory, and is involved in the brain's capacity to access such memories and lay down new long-term memories. So the first and characteristic feature of the disease is memory impairment. For a while at least, your long-term memories, the ones that have been most effectively revisited, or 'overlearned', tend to remain intact. This is because the most well-worn tracks, those of our childhood, for instance, seem to find residence elsewhere in the brain, and so are less affected by the assault on the hippocampus.[5] But as the disease progresses, and the circuits of memory are progressively eroded, more and more of the past becomes inaccessible, and familiar mental routes are simply destroyed.

First the paths of memory fall apart, and then the other functions of the brain. Masses of neurons degenerate, atrophy, and ultimately die. It is like the road to a well-known, well-loved place that has become so broken

33

and obstructed that it is impassable to all traffic, and you can never find your way back, even on foot. Or like a precious library, destroyed by fire.

This image for it is reminiscent of how the horticulturalist and writer Thomas DeBaggio dreams of what is taking place in his own mind. His terrifying, beautiful descriptions of living with Alzheimer's tenderly record the progression of the disease, from the inside: 'I had dreams last night in which fire destroyed my mind, leaving me cleansed and alone.'[6]

In the burning library of the mind, one book after another is destroyed. Rivers shrink and dry up. A great forest is razed. The path to home disappears.

'It's quite frightening, really,' my mother often said.

It seemed like an understatement.

But a lifetime ago in the garden at Blackridge, the mind was still fresh and keen, teeming with new experience, young buds branching into leaf and flower.

'I think it must have been a time of growth . . . of the whole mind, body, spirit,' she told me when I asked her again, another time, what it was that made the place special.

I was still looking for directions, features of the physical landscape that we could use to locate the house. But the most interesting things she said often tended to appear outside the frame of what I'd expected. Again, her answer returned to the child's sensitivity.

'Perhaps it's because your mind is at that ability . . .' she said. 'It was also very emotional.'

'What sort of emotions?'

'The feeling of togetherness taken for granted, togetherness of the family. Everyone was still there. Barts was still there. Jock. Letty got married after that. And you . . . you were just on tiptoe on the edge. You were no longer just somebody in the family. You began to emerge as your own person.'

Blackridge was, in all senses of the word, familiar. A living world in which everyone was together, assembled and at home. But now the other members of her family were all dead and she was confusing me again with Florence, her elder sister whom they called Doodie. The sound of the words, Doodie – Julie, seemed to be enough to do it.

34

'I wasn't actually there, remember? I'm the next generation, your child.'

'Oh,' she looked confused, upset. 'I'll get things sorted out. It shows how mixed up I am.'

'You know, even if your memory gets mixed up, your mind is still as articulate as ever.'

'Yes. Mostly I've got you in the garden, planting things, and watching them grow.'

'And your parents?'

'Well, Dad was busy at the Tech. I remember his blue eyes, and working, digging in the garden, and sitting at the head of the table, and his father and mother. His father faded out very quickly. I don't remember much. He had a white beard.'

After several weeks of tracking, I still had no idea of what I could hope to find at Blackridge. But I knew I had to look. Bring back something growing from the garden.

8.

Two years after the Diamond Jubilee of 1897, young Alan Smallie was besieged in Ladysmith with his regiment, writing letters home.[7]

The presence of two uppity Boer republics near the tip of Africa might have seemed a minor irritation to Victoria's Empire, but there was gold to be had, the industrialisation of a subcontinent to oversee, and a challenge to British authority that should not go unattended. The War was meant to last a couple of months, a straightforward business of dealing with recalcitrant Boers and sorting out the question of supremacy. But the story took a direction that nobody anticipated, and it was nearly three years of conflict before imperial rule over the territory was finally established.

Though my grandfather does appreciate the grit and resilience, even the ingenuity, shown by the enemy, the letters to his parents often return to a sense of bewilderment at the way the Boers were conducting themselves. They were uncivilised, uncouth, and (most significantly) their bottom-up guerrilla tactics involved an outrageously different modality of warfare from what the imperial troops and their generals had had in mind.

'Usually,' he writes, 'when the "capital" of a country has fallen, the war is over, but these semi-barbarians seem to look at warfare in an entirely original way, and go on declaring new "capitals" as fast as they are driven from place to place'.[8]

Instead of unsettling his convictions about power and protocols and civilisation, this peculiar conduct served only to strengthen his commitment to the story of empire that he had enlisted to defend.

It was, of course, a story that had to leave out many things. He must not write too much about the British soldiers dying around him of dysentery and enteric fever, or the young men and the horses torn apart by the guns, or the tens of thousands of black people in supportive roles on either side of the conflict. He must not look too closely at the women and children his men sent to the camps, at the farms and villages that were all burnt out, or at the local people with ancestral claims to the occupied lands. If Liberals in England were accusing their compatriots of barbarism, and of perverting the rules of civilised warfare, my grandfather cannot go this far.[9] But he does keep on writing and paying attention, and he tells some stories that worry at, and even slice right through, the upbeat narratives of his well-fed commanders.

Since letters were censored during the Siege of Ladysmith for fear of the Boers finding out how desperate and insanitary life inside the town really was, he must in particular play down the long bout of enteric fever that nearly killed him. Call it 'the slight attack of fever I had.'[10] Yet he cannot avoid writing about the conditions that made them sick. The plague of flies that overran the town, the simply awful smells, and how messy it was when the Klip River flooded in among men and animals.

Years later when he transcribed the letters, my grandfather added a more frank account of his time in the hospital tent: 'There were absolutely no medical comforts to be had, and scores died from sheer want of proper food and nourishment,' he wrote, describing how he would lie watching as all the dead were collected for burial daily at 10 a.m., the leading body covered with a Union Jack.[11]

If the sanctity of that flag remained intact throughout his life, his impatience with the religion that accompanied it began early. A few months into the War he swiftly dispenses with a sermon that was delivered to the troops by the Bishop of Natal. They were told, he says, that there were two distinct parties in this world (the shepherds and the wolves) and that they must belong entirely to one or the other, that there could be no middle course.

'We must all be either really good or really bad,' he writes. And then goes on, 'I don't agree with this theory though. I am not a shepherd, and I hope I am not a wolf.'[12]

By Christmas of the second year, he notes the irony of celebrating peace and goodwill while, as he puts it, 'we are still trying to slaughter one another, and are not, by any means, practising those precepts and maxims'.[13] The letter does not go on to imagine what it could in fact mean to practise them, but he continues to be a sensitive observer of his fellow human beings, passing on stories to his parents about a great collection of particular people.

Then one evening he tells them about an extraordinary sentence that had just been uttered by one of the cooks, a coolie of Captain Tatham, as he calls him.

'*Ja sahib, kona pudding,*' the man said. And Alan Smallie wrote it down.[14]

Ja sahib, kona pudding. I liked my grandfather for taking note of it: four words, four languages, and a tongue inflected with foreign ships and seas and continents and trade routes and men in uniforms from across the world, a gesture signed all over with the cadences of imperial occupation. If only for a moment, he'd remembered it, a sentence and a supper infused with the voices of a transnational empire, and served by a person who cooked.

Ja sahib, kona pudding. In the story of the South African War that I inherit, this is what remains of a nameless Indian cook who made mealie pudding for the officers in the midst of the Siege, and was, but for this confluence of words, forgotten.

Read together, the mass of my grandfather's letters (slipped through the Siege lines, smuggled past the enemy, carried home from the front on foot, by horse, by train) attest among other things to the unerring efficiency of the colonial postal system, and to the diverse lines of communication and power that kept the Empire going. But if, as one might expect, the correspondence embodied many of the brutal values of the conquerors, what was stranger to me than this was to recognise at the same time the extent of his integrity and the quality of his awareness.

The correspondence depicts a young man who cares for his parents and is kind to the men he commands, who loves his horse Shandy whom he mentions in almost every letter, who is outspoken against pomposity and religious cant, and who strives with an old-fashioned will to be brave, to tell the truth, to do his duty, to work hard.

Again and again, his writing is that of someone whose attention is in the details. The quality of wind on an afternoon in Ladysmith, the state of the failing mealie crop at home when he was not there to plough, the pitiful sight of a convoy of wagons and all their cargo burnt to the ground, the mass of papers he must attend to late at night as the regimental adjutant, the four brief words of a cook.

And ripping through the heart of it is a story from the Siege that lodges like shrapnel in the memory: the bursting shell from a big gun that sliced a young man quite in half.

The letter of Christmas Eve, 1900, begins quite calmly, but goes on to tell about unforgettable things. Smoke and dust, the horrible odour of melinite, the maimed bodies of the dead, the shrieks of the wounded and the plunging horses, and a ninety-pound shell fired from the Long Tom gun on Mbulwana mountain. Young Elliot was quite a boy, he writes, barely seventeen years of age. He did not at first realise that his legs were gone, and repeatedly asked the attendants to bathe his feet. The poor fellow was conscious for some three hours before he died. He was completely cut in two.[15]

A century later, the horror of that letter dislodged a word that returned me to my mother and to another song. The word was Mbulwana.

As a child, I knew the word from the single lullaby she always sang to me at night. The song was in isiZulu, and I did not know what it meant, though I had always believed the last lines were echoing the sound of cannons: '*Kwaduma mbayimbayi / Phansi kwembulwane*.' Over the years I had several times asked isiZulu speakers to translate the song for me, but it had become so eroded in the singing that the meaning was almost unintelligible, like a memory that erases by repetition the vividness of the experience it means to recall.

After reading the letter about young Elliot, I phoned my mother and reminded her about our lullaby. She told me her sister Letty used to sing it to her. Oh yes, she said, it was her song at night, at Blackridge.

When I asked who would have taught Letty the song, she answered in isiZulu, '*Angaas*. There are vast lakes of unknowing in my mind.'

Letty was ten years older than Betty, born in 1908 on a farm in the

39

Dundee district. It was not that far away, geographically, from Lady-smith, and the sound of the cannons during the War would have been fresh in people's memory. So whoever sang the lullaby to Letty (and since her name is irrevocably lost I try to imagine her, a young black woman singing the white farmer's daughter to sleep at night), whoever this forgotten person was, she was singing to the child about recent events, recent trauma, and her song of this war was a tenuous thread stitching through the worlds.

I explained to my mother that I now understood more about the last two lines. That Mbulwana was the mountain outside Ladysmith, and that the cannon, *mbayimbayi*, would have been the big Long Tom that the Boers fired into the town during the Siege.

'Oh,' she said, more interested in the song itself.

And then she began to sing in an old wavering voice on the phone, very tender. The night was huge once more as it was when I was a child, and I could hear the cannons sounding. But my mother was with me in the dark, her voice a thread of love, holding me safe.

9.

An email came in from the Office of the Surveyor General in response to my photograph of the house.

'There are still one or two houses that look like this,' Francois Marais wrote, 'more so towards Braeside Road and not Boughton station. I will take a walk there one day and when you come I could go and show you.'

The ten attachments included some beautifully archaic survey drawings of the area from the 1880s, and a carefully annotated contemporary survey map of the neighbourhood on which he had marked the location of the church and the station, and indicated the position of three likely houses. They looked possible, though their relation to the railway line didn't quite correspond with my mother's descriptions.

The next day he sent an aerial view, with the survey outlines superimposed over it. It was difficult to identify particular houses, but how densely green it looked through the grid. Perhaps the big trees were still there.

His message read simply, 'This may help you find your way.'

10.

As the South African War is coming to an end, Alan Smallie looks back over the three years and considers how much he has changed. He has learnt and seen so much, he writes, and certainly his letters have become more intimate and thoughtful. In the beginning, he explains, I was green. Now I have matured. But while the metaphor he chooses for this story of growing up is an agricultural one, in the final letter he worries that the man he has become will not tolerate a return to the quiet routine of farming life after the campaign is over. He would like to remain a soldier. That was the last letter he transcribed, thirty years later.

But then I found more in the suitcase. In a sheaf of plastic sleeves originally intended for knitting patterns, my mother had filed a batch of letters to his parents that he had chosen to exclude from the official narrative: small folded things written on thick creamy paper, or thin grey-blue paper, or the blue-lined page of an exercise book. Their story is different, a love story.

In the last months of the War when the regiment is encamped at Dundee, Alan Smallie quite suddenly tells his parents about a girl just out of school, the charming, pretty, accomplished Miss Madge Tatham, to whom he is engaged to be married.

After a first attempt at depicting her in words, his next letter says, 'Madge is far better in every way than I described her to you,' and tells how exceedingly popular she is with everyone. The only distress, he writes, is that the days are too short.[16]

For the austere young officer, a man who by the age of twenty-five had risen to the rank of Major 2nd Command of the Regiment, life was now full of dances and garden parties and polo, and even a Sunday school picnic that he willingly attended just because of his darling. He tells how readily her father agreed to his proposal, how warmly the men congratulated him, and writes excitedly of their plans for a life together.

The wedding was two years later, but the letters stop at the end of the war. Except for some comments to his parents about it being time to spruce things up at the farmhouse, in those first happy months of love my grandfather shows no sign of disquiet at the transgression of class that his union with Madge was to commit, or of what its consequences might be. For the Smallies were humble farmers, quite secluded from society, while the Tathams were one of the wealthiest and most influential families in Natal. That the sturdy bearded patriarch WH Tatham (solicitor, estate agent, and first mayor of Dundee) agreed to the marriage at all suggests the extent to which, rising swiftly through the ranks to take command of other men, young Alan had managed to exceed the origins of his birth.

'Yes, she married the most smashing young officer in the regiment,' my mother said when I told her about the uncollected letters. 'I wrote a sentence about it once. It went, "And so they were married, with a great deal of pomp and silverware."'

The love story that the letters tell cannot foresee the years of anxious poverty that were to follow, or the people that Alan and Madge were to be. How, in the collective family memory, the vivacious young girl transformed into Mother, whom all obeyed. Or how the man who could command a regiment was to become what the family called a dreamer.

As for the wedding, apart from my mother's single sentence, I could find no description or even picture of the event, though it must have been a major episode in Dundee society of that year. But then I remembered a photograph that did, in a curious way, record what happened on that day. It was an image not of people, but of wealth: a mass of wedding presents on display on a table. What made the picture of the silverware memorable was the fact that someone had covered all the gifts with a dust cloth, which the hired photographer had omitted to remove.

'Yes,' my mother said, 'it was a photograph of a long table with silver things from end to end, and a white cloth over them, like a sheet. It's very vivid.'

'What sort of things were they?'

'Oh, the teapot, I suppose. All the things that could be silver, the things we used in the house.'

Though he was passionate about his young bride, Alan Smallie probably had little interest in silverware. But in the years to come, the meals he ate with his wife and six children at Blackridge, and in the other houses where they lived, were to offer a daily reminder of the life to which her family was accustomed and for which she had been raised. They were always kept well-polished, my mother said. Spoons, forks, knives, a teapot, last remnants of the Tathams.

'The problem was,' she continued, 'he just couldn't make any money. He thought money was wicked.'

I looked in the family album for the photograph. But it was not there.

11.

In all her stories of Blackridge, my mother would describe her father as a romantic, a man with an aversion to money who loved making things with his hands in his workshop, and who sometimes – even now, seventy years dead – was really still walking on the hill, a small girl beside him in the long green grass.

About her mother, Mary Madeline Smallie née Tatham, she remembered nothing of companionship or ease. Yet a lifetime later the daily presence of my grandmother was constant and unyielding. Mother. After I began looking for the house, one particular story I'd never heard before kept reappearing in different versions.

'Jock had a dog called Bindle,' she told the twins. 'Old Bindle, yes.' She smiled, remembering.

'Then a terrible thing happened one day. My mother said to Jock, "Jock, you must shoot him." So he did.'

What? We were silent.

Then she continued, 'He had to, you see. If my mother had said, "Go and shoot your father," he would have had to do it. Everyone obeyed Mother.'

'Did your father obey her?' Sky asked.

'Well, in a way. Not really. They did love each other, always.'

'Did she love you?' Sophie asked.

'Well, in a way. You know, she had so many children.'

Mother and Dad, the green grass on the hill, the house, the tree, the garden, the railway line, brothers, sisters, dogs, Cyril, the stream. For the present, at least, these things remained clear. And below the hill, near the railway station, the church was present too, a small but resilient structure in the landscape.

After receiving the survey map from Francois, I asked her about it.

'Oh yes,' she said, 'a tiny little church. That was the church we used to go to. I remember Sunday school. I went home and said I was *never* going there again. They used a swear word. Bosom. They talked about Abraham's bosom.'

'Was that considered very bad?' Sophie asked.

'I thought it was terrible.'

'Did you only go once?'

'No, we used to go every Sunday.'

'St Mary's.'

'Yes. I wasn't going to go where they used swear words. Mother played the organ.'

I wrote to the Anglican Archives in Pietermaritzburg about the church. Perhaps there would be some record of the family among the parishioners. Perhaps even an address.

The archivist who swiftly answered my email happened to be Mary Gardner, who was my English teacher at school. She wrote that there had just been a fire in the archive. Because it had run out of oxygen, the fire destroyed very little. But the staff, she said, who'd had to remove all the documents at speed, were now painstakingly going through every single page and trying to brush it clean. The fire had covered the whole collection in soot.

12.

Four years after the end of the War the Natal Carbineers were fighting again, and once more my grandfather was, as he put it, on active service. I learnt this from the other main document in the suitcase, a story of his life written in his early sixties, not long before he died. The tone is formal and characteristically precise about details, dates, and numbers. It is not clear whom the text was intended for, but perhaps, in the face of other family versions, he felt the need to tell his side of things.

Regarding what he refers to as the Native Rebellion and subsequent others have considered to be the beginning of the Armed Struggle, the story he recounts is minimal, almost telegraphic, listing simply the districts where he was involved and the positions he held. Only a single chilling phrase suggests how his particular skills were actually employed in the actions of that terrifying time: 'Press Censor at Nkandla'.[17]

Then, as now still, the deep Nkandla forests were a wild, uncolonised region. A dense ecology of trees and creepers, waters and caves, a world of mists that was crucially inscribed in Zulu history as a place of hiding and surprise attack. So during the so-called Bhambatha Rebellion of 1906, a black uprising against colonial conquest that was catalysed by the Natal government's imposition of a poll tax, it was in these dense forests in the Mome Gorge that Inkosi Bhambatha kaMancinza of the Zondi and his impi took refuge and launched their resistance to the imperial forces. The territory was mountainous and inhospitable to the settlers' volunteer army, and the rebels were elusive, their strongholds hidden in the green. But one morning early, after a tip-off, the colonial soldiers surprised the impi in Mome Gorge and killed nearly everyone, sweeping the ancient forest with fire and ammunition, over and over, killing whoever they could with machine guns, rifles, whichever weapons came to hand.[18]

Alan Smallie, the man of letters, Press Censor at Nkandla, surely saw more terrible things in the decisive massacre of that day than were remembered in the official narrative he must have helped to write. But his part in it all is now untraceable. Perhaps there is some comfort in that. In none of the photographs of men with rifles and Maxim machine guns, moustached men in uniforms, infantry men and men on horses, men with prisoners and men with collaborators, or men marching other men to their death, can I recognise my grandfather. Neither is it recorded how he felt, the farmer's son, grower of mealies and tender of cattle, to be employed in the sickening destruction of people, villages, crops, and animals. For the soldiers not only fought the guerrillas in the forest, but went on to incinerate their lands as they had done during the War, burning homesteads, burning crops, looting livestock, leaving behind them desolation.[19]

The story of his civilian life is told in more emotional detail. After the Rebellion he returned to the farm near Dundee where he had settled with his young bride, in spite of his earlier doubts about farming. But this venture was anything but a success, as he puts it, and when East Coast fever destroyed every last one of his cattle it finally broke him and he was forced to seek employment, taking with him his wife and three young children.

For the next while my grandfather worked as manager or secretary of a series of enterprises of the kind that, after the War, were beginning to open up the Colony to progress and free trade. The fields, the grasslands, and the forests were once again to be laid waste, this time for industrialisation and the factory farms of monoculture. First it was a sugar plantation in New Guelderland, then the Harden Heights Wattle Company, and finally a bark factory on the South Coast that expanded into a fertiliser factory that collapsed before it could go into operation.

His account of it describes the satisfying hard work of organising offices and managing staff. But each time a problem arises, often to do with a difference of opinion with management on a matter of principle (what he calls 'friction'), that makes him move on. Soon after he left the bark factory (where, as he puts it, money was poured out like water, except to the regular employees of the company), he records that the third daughter Betty was born. My mother. He and Madge now had five children, and no prospect of employment. It was, he writes, a decidedly unhappy time.

Then things changed again. The office work he had been doing had taught him how, in theory at least, to run a business, and in 1919 he was offered the job of Lecturer in Book-keeping, Business Methods and Commercial Arithmetic at the Pietermaritzburg Technical College. He was one of six permanent members of staff.

'On the whole,' he writes of the period that followed, 'it was a happy time of just over seven years. We lived at Blackridge and there the third boy of the family was born.'[20]

Those years of my mother's early childhood, when her father had a decent job, a decade or so after what he describes as 'the consummation of Union', were a time when it had already become more important for a certain class of colonials to be 'white' than to be Boer or Brit. After all, as one inspector at the Pietermaritzburg Technicon put it in 1922, 'it is a terrifying thought, yet nevertheless true, that in many avenues of skilled and semi-skilled employment, the coloured can more than hold their own'.[21] Accordingly, the decision was taken to restrict the college to Europeans. In my grandfather's writing there is nothing to suggest he might have objected to this undisguised racism. But he does note that he could not see eye to eye with the principal in all things, and that in the end he tendered his resignation.

My mother remembered this act as yet another moral stand against unscrupulous authority. But what her father wrote was, 'I developed a longing to go back to the land, induced I believe by the experiences I had had of the peculiarities to my mind of many of the people I had come in contact with as an employee.'[22]

Perhaps this inconvenient longing was the reason his family described him as impractical: a man who, after years of regimental service and managerial work, could trade a permanent salaried job in the city for a story of land and the honesty of earth and roots. Could he have forgotten, in this dream of a farm, the cattle destroyed by fever at Dundee, and his own children hungry?

I think he was caught in a net from which farming must have seemed the only escape.

On one hand, the early imprint on his imagination of the story of the British Empire (particularly during the Diamond Jubilee and the South African War, when all his attention was keen and engaged), made it impossible to question the rightness of the imperial project. He appears to have retained throughout his belief in its earth-wide power to rule and to civilise, and his writing tells a story of someone who worked hard to be true to the best of its code of honour.

Yet in practice he had been disappointed. However attentive he may have been as an administrator, by the age of fifty, the man who thought money was wicked had worked in one dreary institution of colonial profit after another (in sugar, timber, bark, even business education) and found that he had had his fill of bosses and the ruthlessness of industry. Another person might have seen another way out. But for Alan Smallie what remained was a yearning for the memory of the thing he had known in the beginning: a place before factories and businesses and wars. The land itself, the farm.

It was 1926 and my mother was eight. Certainly she loved her father. He was such a dear, she always told me, her special person who built beautiful wooden furniture for her dolls, and could swear so imaginatively, and made everything feel all right when they were walking together on the hill.

But his longing to go back to the land was the sentiment that uprooted her world.

After he resigned his job at the Tech, Alan led his family out of the garden at Blackridge and into the desert of a farm on the other side of town: from the green, high-rainfall Mistbelt and the hill to a place of thornveld and stones. They arrived at Umlaas Road just as a long period of drought was setting in, and the years that followed were, by his own account, 'a ghastly business of withering crops and struggling stock'.[23]

Eventually they moved again, and near the end of his life my grandfather was forced to find employment once more. This time he worked as the District Locust Officer in the New Hanover Division, an occupation

which kept him up till dawn supervising the dangerous job of poisoning locusts with sodium arsenite and burning them out with fire.

By day, the red locust swarms of 1934 moved swiftly and terribly
through the land, devouring fields, pastures, and farms like an avenging
army. By night, the District Locust Officer and his staff did battle with
the plague. It was interesting work, dirty work, desperately hard work, he
writes in a description of the exacting use of flamethrowers and poison.
The sodium arsenite, subsequently discontinued, was potentially lethal.
People handling the poison might inhale it or get it on their skin, birds
and grazing animals might ingest it, other plants in the vicinity were
often blighted, the waters contaminated and, like many toxins, the chemical was difficult to store, either corroding or exploding the drums in
which it was held. But the locusts were such a bane to the farmers, and
the authorities so keen to eradicate their invasion, that the deathly impact
of the poison seemed worth the risk.[24]

Locust Officer was the last position he records, but in the heap of
uncollected papers in the suitcase someone had saved one final image
for the story. A yellowing cutting from the *Natal Advertiser* of 1936 shows
a small group of ageing white men in suits gathered convivially around a
big cannon. They are generals, colonels, senators, among them Deneys
Reitz and GMJ Molyneux and, at the centre, chatting, a thin but upright Major AW Smallie. 'Only the Gun Was Neutral!' the headline de-
clares, since this particular gun was used on both sides during the South
African War. The tone is upbeat. For the very weapon that these very
men might well have used to destroy one another a generation before –
a gun just like the cannon on Mbulwana during the Siege – had become
the instrument around which they could now stand together, smiling, in
the redemptive postures of a new supremacy.[25]

My grandfather was asthmatic, and died at sixty-six. It was wartime
again, and the obituary makes much of his medals and his service to the
Empire. I could find no record of the cause of his death, but the brief
account that he wrote of his life concludes with an assertion about the
chemical warfare involved in locust extermination that may have been
premature in its optimism.

His last recorded words are: 'We did not lose a single beast or human being through poisoning. And the poison is really deadly.'[26]

Only the Gun Was Neutral!

Brought together by the Natal Provincial Congress of the United Party, former opponents meet round a gun that was used on both sides during the South African War. It was presented to the Corporation of Durban by the officers of the D.L.I. who received it from Lt.-General Hillyard, Commanding the 5th Division. The words inscribed on it are: "In memory of other days." Those grouped round the cannot, from left to right, are : Col. C. W. Lewis (Natal Police), Col. Deneys Reitz (served on the staff of General Smuts), Col. G. M. J Molyneux (R.D.L.I), Major A. W. Smallie, talking to Col. Molyne··. (Natal Volunteer Composite Regiment) General J. J. Pienaar, on gun (served as Commandant of the Wit· ·rsrand Commando), Senator P. J. Wessels (served on the staff of General Opperman), Senator Col. J. H. ·i·ney (6th Dragoon Guards), and Senator A. J. Spies (adjutant to General Chris. Botha). They are all visitors and delegates to the Provincial Congress.

13.

In the beginning, as she remembered it, things and children grew and flowered according to their nature, roots treading their own paths into the soil. Then all at once people made you brush and plait your hair, and wash your feet, and put on school shoes. Five days a week you had to wear a school hat and a school uniform and carry a brown suitcase full of heavy books and travel all by yourself to town to sit in rows of girls who laughed at jokes you didn't understand in a big building where you didn't know how to use the lavatory and everyone else could do arithmetic and each day began and ended with catching the train.

'It was part of me, I suppose,' my mother said about Blackridge on one of our afternoon visits. 'The awful thing was going to school. Then life became horrible. We had to walk up to the station and go to town by train.'

It was the first break in her life. She was seven, and the family had decided it was time she was properly educated. So she was sent off each day by train to Pietermaritzburg.

The Natal Main Line was a steep metal track that cut right through the green, and the Blackridge station platform was an anxious place, transitional. As you climbed up into the high carriage of the train, you entered a worrying grown-up realm of arrivals and departures between scheduled locations, and became at once a passenger, a body transported across the Colony in a great traffic of goods and other bodies. How small your body felt then. How fast and inexorable the gleaming wheels of the train.

'The railway line was above,' she said. 'The house was on the flat, and then the road wound a little, and then . . . I've got pictures rather than words about the places. You know, I can see the picture, but I can't put it into words.'

'Maybe just now the words part of the brain isn't working as well as the picture part.'

'Yes.'

'And school?'

'The school was Longmarket Street. Walking from the station, sometimes with someone else, but often not . . . Quite a lonely thing for a small child to do. Nobody seemed to worry about that.'

'How old were you?'

'Seven, I suppose. I wasn't terribly happy there.'

The next time she mentioned the train, it was with the same sense of dread.

She said, 'I think our brain takes in certain things, and other things it just passes over. Like going to catch the train. Usually there was an adult with you and you'd go up to the station. And usually there was a tight feeling in your stomach: what happens if the train goes without me? That was a daily thing. The train to the station in town.'

If the journeys by train to school marked the first painful rupture in her life, the decisive eviction from home took place the following year when the family left Blackridge for Umlaas Road. The place was so different that it seemed like another country.

Betty never saw Cyril again.

'He used to always stick out for what he believed,' she said about her father's decision.

'It was easier to love him than your mother,' Sophie said, when she told us again the story of his resignation from the Tech. 'But you did love her.'

'Yes, he was a dear. But yes, I was sort of sorry when she died.'

She went on then to tell us about a little old man with very white hair and the curious name of Mr Gilchrist who was somehow the catalyst for what happened.

'I can't imagine why my father gave it up,' she continued. 'He had a jolly good job at the Tech. Then he left all of a sudden. He had a row with the authorities. They did something to little old Mr Gilchrist.'

'What a name.'

'Yes. My father was quite sure that Mr Gilchrist was in the right. So he

54

had a row with them and left. Then he went to try and farm at Umlaas Road. The silliest thing he ever did.'

Sometimes – if you are born very lucky in this life – there is a grassy hill where you go walking with your father and your brother. There is a garden with mangoes and bananas, and wild leafy places of lichen and moss. There is a stream in the garden, and a best friend to play with. The house has Mother and Father in it, and brothers, sisters, dogs. At dusk the bats come flying.

And then you have to leave.

'It was a little white house,' she said, remembering. 'To us it seemed big, but looking back, it was quite small.'

'And where did you sleep?'

'Oh . . . I suppose with whoever would have me. Letty, I suppose.'

Letty was ten years older and quite grown up. When their own mother was too busy, it was Letty who would love and cuddle her youngest baby sister, mothering her and singing to her at night.

'You remember our lullaby, don't you?' I asked.

I sang the first bit of it, and then she joined in, singing in an old voice.

'What do you think it means?' I was still curious about its meaning. 'You used to tell me the last part was about the sound of the cannons in the Boer war. *Mbayimbayi.*'

'Yes, I think so. I think it's saying something like "Be still, child of my breasts . . ." and then talking about the cannon. But I don't know. Letty would know. She spoke good Zulu.'

'You know what you said when I told you that she had died?'

At the time my mother was eighty and living on her own.

'It was early morning and I came to your flat. You opened the door and you said, "I feel as though the branch I've been sitting on has cracked."'

'So she's dead then, Letty?'

'Yes.'

'And Mother, is she still alive?'

'No, she's dead too. They're all gone now.'

55

14.

The girl who baked mud pies with Cyril grew up to be a teacher. As I listened to her stories of Blackridge, my mother's entire life's work with young children came to seem an affirmation of what she learnt about play and the imagination in those first years before going to school.

At the heart of her teaching was the conviction that every child is creative, and she put aside all predetermined curricula and timetables to help them realise it: the joy of making things, and the beauty of words. After she retired she began to sew quilts and embroideries, stitching bright threads into the forms of leaves, people, animals, birds, suns, a little house. Towards the end she became an old woman in a nursing home bed who wrote poems in a notebook and watched the tree outside, the walls of her room decorated with the nurses' drawings. By the time we began talking about her childhood, her hands could no longer work the needle, and writing had become a struggle. The notebook entries were sparse and difficult to read, and the basket of embroidery silks was a deep tangle of colours lying unused in a cupboard.

As her life unravelled and dissolved into forgetting, I longed for some thread to hold on to. A story, for instance, with plot and characters in it, a journey and a homecoming, paradise and loss, a decisive break with the past after which everything changes. Old as she was, I still wanted these things from my mother, as though by telling stories she might yet hold me in her arms, the daughter she couldn't remember having. But an old woman's stories are fierce shards bound with broken twine. They cannot always give you what you want.

The telephone would ring suddenly and it would be her voice, disturbed with breath and panic, saying, 'I'm shaking all over! I didn't know where you *were* . . .' And then, 'Now where's Mother? And Dad? . . . Why didn't you tell me they had died? . . . At least I don't forget *you*. You didn't die, did you? It makes me feel better to hear your voice.'

Other times, the mind's well-trodden tracks produced situations that seemed crazy in a different way. On one visit not long before we left for Blackridge, I asked what she would like for Christmas.

She answered, 'Something five.'

The twins looked at each other in silence.

'What do you mean?'

'Something five,' she said quite deliberately. 'Five petals, arranged. Two at the top, and three at the bottom.'

Was she talking about a flower? An embroidery design? Perhaps it was just an image, transient as petals, which had floated to the surface in response to the social requirement that she respond to my question. Perhaps it was her old inclination for pattern and form that endured somehow, even as the contents of memory dissolved.

I passed around some biscuits and we fed the pigeons.

Then she began telling a complicated story about someone called Percival who was thrown off a boat for rudeness. At the last minute, Mr Jones, who lived next door, jumped in and saved him.

'His wife, Mrs Jones, was wearing very, very old shoes,' she said.

There was a pause, as we waited for whatever might happen next. Then she added suddenly, 'Pigs keep coming into my mind, followed by hundreds of piglets!'

We all laughed. Who cared, anyway? It was funny. She was enjoying the telling of it, and we were enjoying listening.

The tale wandered on a bit more, and then she finished up rather triumphantly with, 'And then they had to decide who was the bravest one . . . to find out who started this story!'

Sky thought she was teasing us, but Sophie and I were not so sure.

Afterwards, it seemed to me that even in the dreamland of her so-called confusion certain patterns had remained intact: fragments of narrative, the structure of fairy tales, the pacing and inflections of storytelling . . . Whatever else she might have forgotten, these forms were still in place, and they could now be playfully, surrealistically, combined to entertain us.

Clearly she had no interest in gifts that could be wrapped into a parcel. But she could still tell stories. Did she care much, at this late stage, about truth? Make-believe was better now. Pattern and play. Five petals, arranged in order.

15.

An email came in from Andrew Naicker to say he'd discovered that my grandfather's post-war correspondence was housed in the Pietermaritz-burg Archives, having been lodged there by my mother. When I called to ask whether any of the documents from the Blackridge period had an address, I was answered in the deadened voice of official-speak. The woman said she'd get back to me in three weeks' time.

Meanwhile, Andrew visited the Deeds Office and the Office of the Surveyor General in search of the names of property owners. I put him in touch with Francois Marais, and said he should please stop searching at any time if he lost heart or interest, or something else turned up for his attention.

He replied at once, 'I don't think I could quit at this point. Despite my dogged attempts, I just can't seem to source this address.'

Then he wrote saying he was going to have a look around the neigh-bourhood in a few days, adding, 'Something positive is bound to emanate from all this enquiry. It's just a matter of when.' The message ended, 'I suppose we will never really know where we are going until we know where we come from. I will keep looking . . .'

After that, no messages appeared for a while. Then he wrote apologis-ing for not having visited the area yet. There had been a heat wave and he was exhausted. A few days later he emailed saying he had been sick, but hoped to go to Blackridge soon. I enquired further and he explained that he had just been diagnosed with an autoimmune condition that sapped his energy. His email seemed sad and tired, this man I'd never met who had somehow taken on my strange quest as his own. But he managed to end with the brave words: 'I will still try to help you, and hopefully my condition improves to allow me to be more effective and helpful.'

After three weeks, I called the Pietermaritzburg Archives. The woman said that my grandfather's letters in the file were all headed with an address. Each one, that is, except the letters from the Blackridge years.

16.

Just after Christmas, I left for KwaZulu-Natal with Michael and the twins, taking with us on the long drive three photographs, the survey diagrams and satellite pictures, and a dubious assemblage of memories. I had come to accept that neither my mother's stories nor even my grandfather's documents would ever produce a map I could use to find the house.

Instead, all I had was a meandering mesh of paths, people, animals, trees, and fruits. Tracking through the heart of it was a railway line and the Empire for which it was built. And then there was the stream. There had to be a stream.

I called to say a last goodbye before we left, and my mother confused me again with her sister Doodie.

When I corrected her, she said, 'Oh but does it matter?'

'No it doesn't.'

Who is alive anyway? I wondered. And who is dead?

She laughed and said, 'You could write a book with that title, you know: *Does it Matter?* You'd find that most things don't.'

THE HOUSE

1.

On the road. Driving through. Back. All the way back. Back home. Going home. Maybe.

There is something compelling about a long car trip. The maps, the packing, the padkos, the space of a day or more extracted from usual time to do this single thing, this journey, thin line of road travelling through the vastness of rock and veld and sky, small remnant wildness on either side between tar and fenced field, broken bottles tossed and glinting among stones, the silence, the conversation, the long hours of simply driving, the designated concrete picnic spots where we seldom have lunch, the interchangeable one-stop plastic-neon garage shops stacked with instant comfort, the blue mountains layered like tissue paper into the horizon, the empty sky traced with birds and clouds, the ancient grass-lands, the silent rocks, the gravel track with its potholes and pale dust, the open road, the national highway, freight of meek sheep travelling double-decker to the slaughter, trucks laden with logs and petrol and sugar and cooking oil and dead birds, the school bus packed with skinny children in the afternoons, each one of us held fast and fragile in a capsule of steel on a narrow track through the world, vector of carbon and transport and trade and more carbon, placeless and displaced, driving and being driven, silence and sitting still, wondering, wandering, meandering, empty sky blue mountains wide grasslands deep rocks, this world glimpsed for a breath perhaps, for a day (a hawk circles overhead, a cloud of finches flies up from the warm tar, a crow pecks at roadkill), this world through which we're passing, small urban humans on the road again, in transit, crossing over, some new quest.

We left home before dawn, taking the N1 out of Cape Town and spending the night at Hanover in the Karoo. The owner of the Victorian guest house said he used to live in the city, but now at last he'd found a place where he belonged.

'*Mense sê as jy in die Karoo kom bly is jy mal. Maar you know, it's really lekker here. Hier bly ons vreeslik lekker.*'

It was something he might well say to every guest, but his smile was convincing, and we followed his advice to take a back road from Bloemfontein around the edge of Lesotho into KwaZulu-Natal.

'It's more scenic,' he said. 'It's a longer way around and it's slower, but you'll enjoy it.'

The twins in the back seat found the second day's journey interminable ('Why can't we fly?' they moaned. 'Or at least take the national road?'). But after the fast-paced freeway I was glad of a wandering dirt road, happy to pass through slow villages that the N1 had forgotten, houses built in a time when a person might spend weeks carving a gatepost out of teak, as though to say, 'This is it. This is the place. I'm not going anywhere.'

And the back roads had people in them. A small girl in a floral dress was riding a bicycle. A young man was walking at midday on the R26 from the direction of Maseru. And high in the Maluti mountains, an elderly man was sitting on the side of the road, selling small clay pots.

'Who made them?' I asked.

'Me and my wife.'

When you're looking for something, you tend to find traces wherever you go: red ochre clay dug out of the hill, formed by warm hands, decorated with fine lines, burnished and fired in a grass oven. The little pot I bought from him for my mother evoked a yearning for something I could not name.

Back on the highway to the Natal Midlands, we returned to the thundering corridor of steel and carbon before taking the turnoff to Mooi River. The plan was to break the journey to Blackridge with a few days' stay on a farm. Or rather, the Hoek was not *a* farm, but *the* farm. The place where Michael's family, the Copes, had lived for a hundred years. He had not been there since childhood, but a new owner had recently turned it into a self-catering guest house, and it was possible to visit again, though in circumstances in which familiarity and strangeness were likely to be inextricable.

It was another story of home and dislocation, memory and forgetting. But this house, the place they'd now renamed De Hoek House, was perfectly real and precisely located. I called out the directions from the website as we turned off the N1 into a country road which turned into a farm road which became a dirt track down a steep hill through high grass and late-afternoon weaver birds which finally led to a newly painted gate.

At the threshold was an oak tree, heavy with green summer.

2.

'Look, there's Granny Cope's tree,' Michael called out as we drove through the gate towards the farmhouse.

The oak just inside the electric fence was massive, planted in the late 1870s by the twins' great-great-grandmother Frances. Like my grandmother Madge Tatham, Frances Stocker was an upper-middle-class girl who fell in love with a farmer. But where Madge's father was glad to endorse the marriage to Alan Smallie – or at least in the beginning – the Reverend Stocker, Oxford-educated rector of a comfortable parish in Staffordshire, refused to countenance his daughter marrying below her station.

What happened next was a transgressive act of love and determination that eventually led to the occupation of this farm, and became the defining moment in Michael's family story. Frances was a dutiful Christian daughter and her father's favourite. But like a brave girl in an old ballad she made the break, and eloped with the farmer John Cope across the sea to Canada. Her father never forgave her, and when he finally died, she was cut off in his will with a shilling. Her sister Emily tried to share her own substantial inheritance with Frances, but Frances was too proud to accept it. So Emily bought a farm in the Colony of Natal as a christening present for the youngest son, baby Carol. This Frances could not refuse.

And so it happened that in 1874 she made the long sea passage via England with her husband and three young sons, and arrived at a place in the world called Mooi River, acorns from home in her pocket.

The residence they built at the Hoek was big, a solid, beautiful thing made of stone and wood and glass to last for many generations. As we stood before it that afternoon, my mother's little wood-and-iron house became even less substantial than before, like the wistful leavings of a dream.

The owner welcomed us warmly. Yes, he knew of Frances. A previous occupant used to see her walking through the great central corridor at night. But he was a bit mad, they said. Boarded up the moulded ceilings with false ones made of pine floorboards so he'd be able to hide in the gap when the blacks came to kill him, and burnt the family books and papers that he found in the cellar.

Luckily, the manuscript was discovered before that: her novel. When Jack Cope excavated the bundle of papers from an age of forgotten documents, the first five sheets were gone and an unknown number missing from the end. What remained were five hundred pages written in a fine cursive hand not unlike my grandfather's, though the book Frances had written trusted the imagination more than his writing did. My ring-bound photocopy of the text was a weighty thing, but it seemed likely to have some resonance with the Blackridge story. And if ever I was going to read it, this had to be the place.

We crossed the lawn to the verandah. It was all kikuyu, radiant in the late sun.

'Too coarse and bright,' Michael said.

Instead, what he remembered was Granny Cope's fine green lawn cut neat around the fountain. And while the oak tree still stood at the portal where she had planted it, the farm of his memory was made of long days swimming in the river, big rooms peopled with stories, and the front hill branded with lightning and death. Now one side of the verandah had been enclosed to build an en suite bathroom for the master bedroom, and the kitchen had been moved and remodelled. And when he looked for the tall mixed conifer forest that John Cope had planted with seeds brought from Canada, it was gone.

'It's wrong,' he said. 'It's all wrong.'

Yet each time he crossed the threshold, arms laden with things from the car, he would stop.

'I know this smell. This is what the Hoek smells like. I would know this smell with my eyes shut. Anywhere.'

3.

The novel Frances wrote begins in the old kitchen, but the homely tale it tells about love and community is yet another story of war.

On the first page that's left of the manuscript, family dogs and a pet lamb called Waterloo bound into a crowded room, the lamb is fed porridge and milk, and the small children of the family are told to wash their hands before tea. The next day after breakfast they all take the pony up to the main road to watch soldiers marching by. This is the treat the little ones have been begging for, but there is a shadow to the day's excitement. As Frances describes it, the brave Englishmen are 'going to give their lives, it might be, in that savage Zulu war for the preservation of so many families in this land of their adoption.'[27] Within days, the farm receives the news of the Battle of Isandlwana.

The title page is gone, but I came to think of the book as *Koppie's Story*. Like Frances Cope, the main character Margaret Coates lives with her family on a beautiful farm in the Natal Midlands. Her mother has died, and as the eldest daughter she must take care of both her father and numerous siblings. They call her Koppie because she is like a small hill that is rough and strong. Like Frances again, she loves a man whom her father would never consent for her to marry. But where Frances defied the old rector, and this defiance was the single act for which she was most clearly remembered, Koppie is obedient to propriety in this matter of the heart, and it is not until the very end of the book that she glimpses another possibility.

So goes the framing story, a sentimental tale. Reading it each day at the Hoek, it became clear that what really interested Frances was not plot but subtext: the intimate world of this farm, or one very like it, a dense mesh of distinctly unsentimental stories about a life of women's work and women's joy and pain, a tough and tender domestic universe

70

of children, servants, animals, recipes, and plants. But for all this particularity, the intricate world of the farm is situated at a critical historical moment. And while for Koppie the domestic sphere is at the heart of things, she cannot but feel the reverberations of the battles being fought further afield to secure the occupation of the land by people like her family. And, of course, my own.

It was a pivotal moment for everyone in the region. Transitional. By early January 1879 when the Redcoats marched past the farm on their way north, Natal had for some months been assembling wagons, troops, and ideological ammunition for a brutal war against the amaZulu. The time was overdue (at least that is what they said, some of the colonial authorities, notably Sir Bartle Frere, the British High Commissioner) for the substantial power of the Zulu Kingdom to be dismantled. For as long as the territory of King Cetshwayo kaMpande and his people remained independent of British rule, white settlers would be at risk from black savages. Or so they said. More to the point, the commercial and political interests of Victoria's Empire – which required that Zulu labour and Zulu land be brought into service of the Colony's developing capitalist economy – would be restricted. So when the king refused to accede to an ultimatum whose terms would have amounted to subjugation, this was used as a pretext for the invasion of Zululand. The battles that followed were decisive, the human suffering immense, and the long-term socio-environmental impact of the invasion catastrophic. Before the year was up, the kingdom had been conquered, resistance quelled, and Cetshwayo himself led into exile.[28]

Koppie's Story starts at the beginning of this critical year and goes on into 1880.

In the novel, Frances records the imprint of these ongoing wars of occupation from a domestic vantage point. While she still feels exiled by the unhealed wound of her father's wrath, she does what she can to give herself wholeheartedly to the intense life of a farm in the Colony. Inevitably, the book she writes is a story of home: the threads and seeds and stories that still bind the family to England, and the minute particulars of making a settler's life in another place.

So Koppie worries about money, she labours to make beautiful butters for the agricultural show, and she bakes breads and rabbit pie. Frances describes how they shell mealies on the farm, and how one day little Toby's hand gets caught in the blade and Koppie bathes the tiny fingers, binding them up separately and saturating the bandage with Arnica. She shares with her readers the joy of the garden in the early morning, the panic of a child's croup in the middle of the night, the comfort of the hills and the spruit and the rocks and wild flowers, and how on Queen Victoria's birthday the family goes for a picnic up in the hills, singing 'God Save the Queen' before the meal instead of the usual hymn. There is a story about a disselboom breaking, a hut that catches alight, stories about following the song of a honey bird all the way to the comb, and about a porcupine hunt, and what the different thorn trees are and how they may be used, and how Koppie loves botanising and digging up plants in the veld to take home. She tells about Esther's new doll, and various kinds of mistletoe, and eating flying ants, and how to stamp clothes or make cake in a baking pot over a fire in the veld, scraping soda off a rock to make the dough rise. And there's a story about the buck that eat cabbages, and about visiting a shepherd's wife in her grass hut when she is sick with *umkuhlane*, while the other women sit around her sickbed talking, just like the cottagers in England do when someone is ill.

The effect is a dense embroidery of stories, women's tales of place. And meshed into this fabric, the big events of history are told with the same intimacy.

A few days after the ominous spectacle of the queen's soldiers at the opening of the novel, the sky suddenly begins to darken and everyone on the farm is bewildered. They are all helping to dip the sheep for an infection of scab in a great bath of warm water infused with tobacco and sulphur when the partial solar eclipse begins. Later, the Coates family's midday meal is disrupted as the children try to watch the eclipse through soot-blackened glass. Frances writes that the workers are frightened that the sun is hiding his face.

The darkness certainly felt momentous, but nobody on the farm could have imagined what it would later come to signify. The day of the dead moon, the day the sun turned black, was the day of the Battle of Isandl-wana, the twenty-second of January. Within two hours, King Cetshwayo's warriors defeated the invading British forces and their African levies, leaving only a handful of men alive. In the nightmare months that fol-lowed, as the Colony called for vengeance and the coherence of the Zulu nation was systematically taken apart, the darkening of the sky at the height of the battle seemed for both sides like a portent of disaster.

Once the news reaches Koppie's district, panic spreads among the farmers about whether to flee or stay. Like other settlers in the Colony, they fear that a Zulu army is on its way to attack them. But what is striking about Frances's description in the novel is the way it puts aside that terror. In her story of the battle, the people who are suffering most are black.

A tall, semi-nude man came into the dining room, she writes, followed by about seven others. The Coates family are discussing the British losses at Isandlwana, and considering whether to stay or leave. But their con-versation is silenced by the anguish of the farm workers who have lost family members in the battle.

'They entered and arranged themselves along the wall of the room in perfect silence, with dejected countenances, heads bent down and their arms crossed upon their breasts. When they spoke it was with one voice: "Our Fathers and Brothers are all slain! We want to go to our kraals. Dead – dead – they are all dead!" and their voices sank into a low wail.'[29]

4.

If, as they say, any war lasts three generations once the fighting is over, what might it feel like to live in peace?

Still, a hundred and thirty years later when we visited the Hoek, the horror of that time seemed almost forgotten. After the long drive from Cape Town, and the long anguish of the nursing home, the farm entered the mind like a balm. The house was solid, a live thing made by human bodies and the workings of insects, mice, and birds: each stone cut from rocks on the hill, each settled window frame sawed by living hands, the slow curve of a floral design carved in yellowwood, the flesh of great trees, golden.

One twin wrote in her diary, splashed in the stream, and painted a picture of the oak tree to send home as a postcard to Granny. The other watched a mouse in its nest, and did battle with the invasive black wattles that his paternal ancestors planted. I baked scones – the wide verandah seemed to call for it – and read *Koppie's Story*, while Michael made carvings from pine bark, painted watercolours, and during a fierce electric storm told the story of Jack's own twin brother Tom who was killed by lightning on the front hill at the age of twenty-one. As a child my mother taught me to love a summer thunderstorm, calling me to the window to watch the sky, and afterwards taking me outside to smell the rain. But on the farm the lightning was different, charged forever with the death of a beloved twin.

All day the swallows flew in and out of their mud house, and we savoured the taste of a familiar longing: back to the land. But Michael was full of a child's precise recall of how things used to be, and how they'd changed, tugged between love, nostalgia, and disquiet.

At last he said, 'It's a theme park of itself.'

74

I could recognise it then in the stillness of the place, the very absence of busyness that made it feel peaceful. In Koppie's day, and even in Michael's memory, the farm was a hamlet of activity, a place where all the human people work hard all day, sustaining a difficult life in a domestic world shared with dogs, ducks, sheep, cattle, horses, and a particular canary. Now the stone fountain was gone, the old forge was in ruins, the dairy had been converted into an extra set of guest bedrooms, the milk cows replaced with the neighbour's low-maintenance beef cattle, and – probably for the first time ever in all the years that our species have lived in the region – there were no dogs.

At night it was very dark, beautifully so. But again, for the first time in generations, it was a darkness no longer lit by human hearths. Before the Copes' hundred-year tenure, a trekker called Rudolph occupied the land and named it Rudolph's Hoek. And before that? By the time we visited, the only person living permanently on the farm was a man who introduced himself simply as Sicelo. He was reticent at first, but open to talk. His grandfather used to work for Mr Cope, he said, and after a bit of questioning he told how, in recent years, he himself had been ordered to pull down the old cottage and cut down the mixed conifer forest that John Cope had planted. Now his main work was tending the flower garden and the swimming pool. Keeping the grass neat.

On late afternoons while he did so, I sat reading about the kraals, the mealie gardens, the thin dogs, and the cultural practices of his ancestors who lived in this valley that the settlers had come to own. Unsurprisingly, Frances assumes black people to be servants, and believes they need religious education. But while many settler narratives have little interest in the lives of the human beings who work for them, she can tell you how a particular species of stick that grows in the Thorn Country is bent and interlaced to make the frame of what she calls a beehive hut, how the frame must be thatched with a grass named *isiqunga*, and how the women pound anthills with smooth river stones for the floor, squirting water from their mouths to soften the clay to make a surface that is smooth and polished as marble.

By contrast with the prissy and naïve racism of her visiting friend from the city, Koppie is relentlessly curious and attentive. She finds the young women adorned with beads and carrying baskets of oranges on their heads picturesque, the African wedding that the family attends is a fascinating spectacle, she records in detail the shields, assegais, skins, belts, beadwork collars, and bunches of long black tail feathers from the sakabula hanging from the roof of the huts, and the woodwork that becomes black and shiny from the fire. In her telling of it, the world she describes may be timeless and exotic, but she is not unsympathetic.

And then at certain moments the real pain of real human beings ruptures this gloss. The first time is when the tall men come to the Coates's dining room after Isandlwana. The second is when she visits the kraal of a chief who lives in the Thorn Country, where her family has grazing lands.

Inkosi Phakade kaMacingwane of the amaChunu, whom she calls Chief Pagadi, was familiar with white visitors, and there was a period when he was something of a favourite with Theophilus Shepstone, the influential Colonial Secretary for Native Affairs. Like that of other so-called loyal chiefs, his position gave the colonial administration a means of indirect rule and a buffer against the Zulu kingdom. In those early years the chief, who had drawn some benefit from the colonial presence, would lay on colourful ceremonies at his homestead for visiting dignitaries, among them Bishop Colenso and H. Rider Haggard, who both wrote about the experience.[30]

But this was all before Isandlwana. On that day of the dark sun, he lost three sons, among them his heir. Immediately afterwards, his two grandsons were killed at Rorke's Drift. All of them died defending the Colony, so to speak, from the amaZulu.

When Koppie meets Chief Pagadi, it is later in the same year. Suddenly he has become an old man.

Her uncle asks him if it is well with him, and he answers, 'How can you ask if it is well with me when my sons are not, and my sons' sons are not, and my people are not? They all rest at Isandlwana.'

When the uncle persists, saying he was asking after the chief's health, he replies, 'Oh yes, I am as well as a sorrowing man can be.'[31]

The chief's despair is palpable from Frances's description, even if she cannot know the full tragedy of his relationship with the colonial administration. After the terrible conflicts of 1879, in which British forces assaulted both the military power of the Zulu kingdom and the sustainability of the homestead economy, it was no longer necessary to have chiefs like Inkosi Phakade to act as collaborators, or to put on shows of tribal dancing.

As Frances correctly records, he died the following year, a man living on the cusp.

5.

Perhaps home is always a story of displacement and return and displacement again. An old track played on repeat.

By 1880, when *Koppie's Story* ends, the Empire had invaded Zululand and the Natal Government Railways line had reached as far as Pietermaritzburg, on its way into the continent. By the following year, when the first train arrived at a tiny station they named Swartkop, later known as Blackridge, something irrevocable had taken place. With the human inhabitants of the Colony now somewhat under control, the stage was set for the settlers to escalate the war to another level: a battle with the forests, the grassland, the rivers, and the non-human people who had always lived there.[32]

The Hoek was one of the many beautiful farms in the Natal Midlands where they established this occupation of the land. But by the time we visited, it was poised at another critical moment. The owner explained that the old dairy farming model was no longer sustainable, and that he planned to combine with neighbouring farms to make a game reserve. In other words, for the first time ever the land was in possession of a globalised class of *Homo sapiens* who had the means and the education to choose neither to farm nor to hunt. Already some of the wild ones were coming back.

The birds, of course, had never really left. In the afternoons, I'd drive up to the hill to call my mother on the cellphone, and talk about birds. She was lonely, she said, but she still had the pigeons.

'There's a brown hawk up here watching me from a post,' I told her.

'There was always a hawk,' she said. 'At Blackridge.'

I told her about the swallows' nest in the verandah roof, and the doves and pigeons that called and called, the mass of red bishops and weaver birds in the reeds, and how in the mornings when it was misty you would hear the rainbird.

'*uFukwe*,' she said immediately, the isiZulu name for Burchell's Coucal.

It's a big brown bird, seldom seen. But that liquid voice is unmistakeable. When I was a child, she especially loved *uFukwe*.

'Come and listen,' she would call me quietly to the garden. 'It's going to rain.'

'And what about sakabulas?' I said, 'You remember them? Lots up here in the field. The twins thought they were a giant dragonfly.'

'Of course! Black and glossy. And that long long tail. We used to watch them flying over the high grasses on the hill. You'd think that tail would pull them down to earth, but it never did.'

The farm was full of birdsong, but in all the singing of those few days there was one three-note call I'd not heard for years, and it reached instantly into a forgotten, wordless memory of summer. Piet-my-vrou, the Red-chested Cuckoo.

'Whipoorwill,' my mother said when I sang the call for her on the phone. 'So lovely.'[33]

'In isiZulu it's *uphezukomkhono*,' Michael remembered. 'Jack used to say it means something like "shoulder the hoes". It's a migratory bird, so when you hear it calling again in spring, you know it's time to start ploughing.'

Now there was nobody left on the farm to be reminded to plough, and the new paying guests like ourselves wanted ecotourism.

It would have been a curious concept for Frances and her self-sufficient family. In her novel, the Coates family are pioneers who know domestic animals intimately as either friends or food. But the wild ones are game, prey, vermin, the excitement of the hunt, and the men enjoy killing them with their guns and sticks and dogs. Koppie's brothers kill buck for meat, and they kill porcupines when they eat the mealies. They kill an antbear just to show her what it looks like (she says it is naked, with a long thin snout, and extraordinary paws, like hands). And one morning when the brothers find a mother jackal and her cubs who are sleeping in their burrow, they kill them too. Frances explains that the species is what is called the maned jackal because of the long hair on their necks and backs which stands erect when they run. They are smaller, she says, than the common jackal, and in shape and motion greatly resemble the hyena. Their hair is rather long, of a yellowish colour prettily striped with black. Her description is characteristically attentive, almost tender, a precise account of an animal that is in fact not a jackal at all, and not even carnivorous. The aardwolf, whose shaggy appearance has often led farmers to mistake it for a predator, eats insects, mostly termites. Frances describes how the cubs they found in the burrow were young, about the size of a full-grown cat. Except for one that escaped, Koppie's brothers and their dogs killed them all, after a desperate fight with their mother.

In all these images of destruction there is just one brief moment when Koppie, looking at the body of a buck the men have shot, feels some remorse at its grace and beauty. 'I feel sorry,' she says, 'to see them lying dead. But in the excitement of the chase I feel no pity.'[34]

After reading one such story after another, it was comforting to see reedbuck quietly grazing on the hill. One morning a pair of aardwolf appeared suddenly from the cover of a bush to run towards the river. And early one evening, a low movement ran along the inside of the electric fence. The gait was distinctive, trotting. A jackal, black-backed. There he was, or she. Tracking through the land again, checking things out.

6.

On our last day at the farm we made a picnic beneath the oak tree, a green so dense with life that it was dark at noon. The children gathered acorns – alien seeds, I thought, ancestors – while Michael set the sailing boat he'd made from ponderosa pine bark to float on the swimming pool, and lodged the face he'd carved in the fork of a branch, looking out towards the river. I wandered into the field beyond the fence, knee-deep in flowers and summer grasses, remembering English folk songs.

When I called my mother, I told her we'd be at Blackridge the next day.

'That's lovely,' she said. 'Take me with you.'

'We will. In our minds.'

'Yes, that's what I mean.'

Next morning, I felt a sudden desire to take back with us one of the oak saplings that had sprouted near Granny Cope's tree. Sicelo brought a spade, came over to help. I'd have liked to dig the little tree out myself, but he was strong and insistent. Kind.

'I'll do it,' he said, flash of cowhide bracelet on the wrist as he dug.

There was probably too much history between us for it to be otherwise. As on every other day, the birds sang continually, an ancient thread of song, as yet unbroken.

7.

'Do you feel at home yet?' the twins asked as we descended the hill into Pietermaritzburg. It was, after all, my home town, too, though curiously I'd never been to Blackridge, and when I was growing up it was not something my mother had thought of doing.

'And now?'

When Francois Marais had suggested we meet at the old railway bridge, it seemed like just the right place. In all my mother's stories, the railway was the neighbourhood's defining thoroughfare. Below the line, above the line, this side of the tracks and that: the world she knew first was divided into regions by the narrow-gauge track, and the great steam locomotive powering through the green. Now in old age the railway line had returned to track through her dreams, and she would call in a panic, convinced she was in the carriage of a train again, stomach tightened with fear.

'I need your help urgently!' she might say, breathless on the other end of the phone. 'I'm on a train and I don't know where to get off!' Or other times, slightly formally, 'Hello, I'm here on a train and I need to be sure there's someone to meet me at the station.' Or else simply, desperately, 'You've got to come and meet me now, the train's arriving soon!'

At first, I'd try reasoning with her. 'Have a look around,' I'd say in a tone that must have sounded patronising, 'It's your own room, not a train.'

But Sky, who phoned his grandmother every day to chat, knew better what was needed to help her relax.

'Okay fine,' he'd say in an easy voice. 'We'll be there to meet you. Don't worry.'

In the early 1880s the arrival of the Natal Government Railways from Pietermaritzburg gave rise to the little station they called Swartkop (later

Blackridge), and the particular line that the train took through the territory came to define all subsequent lines. The Mistbelt patchwork of grassland-and-forest environment was surveyed, more lines were drawn on maps, money changed hands, and on either side of the tracks properties began to appear. As the Natal Main Line made it through to the interior, the iron-and-timber track laid piece by piece across the land swiftly became the vital artery of Empire and the coal-powered train its vehicle. While in 1880 Koppie must travel to Pietermaritzburg by ox wagon, and then take the train the rest of the way to Durban, by the time Alan Smallie was writing letters home from the Siege in Ladysmith, the track reached all the way from the coast to the Witwatersrand, and a great traffic of coal, timber, metal, cattle, farm produce, soldiers, workers, fortune-seekers, and administrators was being conveyed across the Colony and across the globe as never before. Shipping lines, railway lines, lines of command: to the occupying powers, it must have seemed unassailable.

So for various reasons it made sense to begin my search at the railway bridge. Francois was waiting for us on the grass on the lower side of the embankment. He wore a pale-blue open-necked shirt, a middle-aged man with a sensitive face. As we got out of the car to greet him, I saw what should have been obvious from the research I'd done in Cape Town.

The railway line itself had completely disappeared.

It was one of those moments that seems in retrospect to have been significant, but is difficult to absorb at the time. I was quietly astonished: first by the fact that the vanished line had been replaced by a wide expanse of grass and flowers that led through the heart of the neighbourhood, and then by my own denial of the evidence. It had, of course, been clearly visible in the Google maps and satellite photographs, which depicted the old railway servitude as an open space, abandoned after the line was rerouted to a less steep gradient. But, like my mother lying in the nursing home bed and insisting she could still walk and take care of herself, I'd cared so much about the idea of that line that I'd been unable to recognise that it had gone.

Francois smiled and we shook hands. His eyes were kind.

'Come,' he said, 'let's walk and I'll show you some houses. There are a couple that just might be the one. We can compare them with the photograph you sent me.'

It was drizzling, fine Mistbelt rain, and soon we were all wet and muddy, up to our knees in the rainy grass of the wide green path where the railway used to be. On the left, the dark shape of the hill loomed like an old giant high above our heads: the black Ridge itself, guardian of dreams and nightmares, disappearing into cloud like mountains in China. And on either side of the grassy railway servitude grew wildness and immensely high trees, so that walking together in the misty rain of a late afternoon in high summer we entered a lush realm of green and more green.

'A hundred colours all called green.'

It was my mother's voice in my head, what she'd often say to me as she looked out at the garden from her bed in the nursing home, uttering the same words each time as though it were the first. I knew then that I would recognise the house when I found it.

After a few minutes' walking, Francois pointed above the railway line to a white cottage with a tin roof.

'You think that could be the one?'

'No.' I felt certain. 'It's from the same period, but the shape's not right. And it's too high up there as well, and above the line. She always says it was below.'

Next to it was another house with Cape Dutch gables, moulded pillars, high security fence. Too big.

'Well,' Francois said, 'I think those two are the only old ones around this part. But I can show you a couple of others further down the hill near the newer railway line.'

We turned back towards the car. It was raining harder, and our long pants were soaked. The twins' patience was beginning to wear out.

'And what about the other side of the old railway line up here?' I asked. 'We've been looking for the house above the line, but what about below? This old line would have been the one she knew, and it's what she always talks about. She says the house was below it.'

'I don't think so,' he said. 'But you can't be sure. The trees are so tall.'

84

We peered into a few of the properties below the railway servitude, but the mesh of green was so deep that it was impossible to see far beyond the fence. Back at the bridge everyone climbed into the old Golf that Francois was driving.

'Look,' I said, 'your keys!' He had left them in the ignition.

He laughed, 'You know I quite often do that. Sometimes the car doesn't start too well if you take the keys out.'

The other two houses he wanted to show us were a way down the hill near the new railway line. I knew at once they were wrong. Both were old, yes, but built of brick, not wood and iron. The gardens were small, planted with high palms, lawns, and hydrangeas. Big dogs, angry ones, tried to attack us from behind the electric fence, and Sky provoked them to even more fury, jumping about and waving his arms. I just wanted to go away. Not this. Not brick.

Francois walked on a bit further, protecting his printout of my photograph from the rain as best he could. But he had shown me all he could think of, and everyone was tired and wet and cold. I thanked him and we said goodbye.

'Please let me know if there's anything else.'

'Thank you again, Francois. So much. You've been so kind.'

The rest of the family were eager to get back into the car. But the walk had unsettled me, and I set off barefoot in the rain for a last look around.

In an undeveloped plot below the old line was a great stand of wild bananas. Maybe the bats were still there, the baby bats asleep in a curled leaf.

8.

'Would you like some hot chocolate?'

It was Mary Gardner, speaking to the wet children as we crossed the threshold.

'Yes please!'

The thought of hot chocolate was a perfect one, and with it we settled at once into the warmth of the Gardners' hospitality. After raising five children and taking care of numerous other people in that rambling Victorian house, Mary (my English teacher at school) and Colin (my English professor at university) knew how to look after you.

Their home was in Prestbury, a little way down the hill from Black-ridge, and they had invited us to stay for a few days while I pursued my quest. Probably there was a time when the big rooms and wide verandah built of the gentle apricot-red brick that characterises the old buildings in Pietermaritzburg housed the genteel social rituals of a confident ruling class. But after forty years of family, friends, animals, poems, stories, meals, and progressive ideas, the house had long outgrown its colonial origins, while the large garden had become a forest of massive avocado trees and mangoes, abundant ferns and mosses, all splashed with rain.

Before these recent incursions, the archaeological record shows that people have been living in the area for at least half a million years. For while there is no mention of Blackridge on the current maps of Stone Age sites, the neighbourhood now known as Prestbury is one of the places where modern humans have found stone tools: artefacts that date all the way back from the recent tiny arrow points and scrapers used by the last hunter-gatherers to the weighty hand-axes of the Early Stone Age.

On a previous visit, Colin had endeared himself forever to Sophie and

Sky by cheerfully explaining to them, in his characteristic lisp, the simple rules of the house: 'No rules. No restrictions.'

This time, laughing as he showed us to our rooms, he told us, 'One guest said what she really liked about our house was that it was so shabby!'

'We call it a wilderness garden now,' he went on with a mischievous smile when we took a walk around the garden. 'People ask how we got it like this!'

'Well,' I said, 'I like people with this sort of garden.'

Next morning, I woke before dawn from a dream in which a very old woman, not in fact my mother, was slipping down a cliff, slipping and screaming, reaching out. Her daughter had given up, and was walking to the bottom to collect the body. But I told Michael to grab her hands, and I took his feet, and somehow we pulled her up. Back from the brink, an old tale. But who was it that was falling, and who was being saved?

Pondering the dream in the dark, I could feel the generous mind of the house was awake too, thronged with dreams and stories, a whispering library of books in every room. The elderly hardcover volumes consigned to our guest bedroom were not central any more, if they ever had been, but kept safe nevertheless, like memories whose trace might yet hold you fast, remember you when you forget: *W.B. Yeats*, and *Yeats' Blessing on Von Hugel: Essays on Literature and Religion*, and *A Review of Soviet Literature*, and *Famous Poems* ... The evening before, Colin had told us about a friend who got rid of most of his books, and then spent the next two years trying to buy them back from second-hand shops.

For breakfast Mary brought out mangoes and paw-paws and lady-finger bananas, and I told them about the mango tree in my mother's garden.

'It's a good climbing tree, yes,' Mary said. 'And we used to pick lots of mangoes from ours. But now the monkeys get most of them. And the other fruit too.'

Monkeys. If you don't have to live with them, you probably love them. When I was growing up in Pietermaritzburg, you might occasionally have the treat of seeing vervet monkeys on a visit to Wylie Park or the

Botanical Gardens. But in recent years they'd begun appearing in green spaces all over the city: mothers entering the suburbs with babies on their backs or shepherding a playgroup of toddlers, adolescents skittering and preening, young males chancing their luck with the kitchen.

'It's sort of *The Empire Writes Back*,' Colin said, with a smile.

He explained that when the family moved into the house in 1965 there'd been no monkeys. Then a few appeared, rather shyly, some years later. But once the City turned the plantation behind the house into a neat suburb, they disappeared.

'Then about ten or twelve years ago they began to come back,' he said. 'At first shyly, but now very confidently. Now they sometimes look at us as though we had no right to be here.'

Of course, however much you like them, monkeys are a nuisance to the priorities of human primates. In KwaZulu-Natal the vervets have been increasingly turning up in the cities to look for food, as the office parks, shopping malls, golf estates, and gated communities of *Homo sapiens* sprawl into regions where the little primates used to live. The human activists who are on their side tell terrible stories of people shooting, poisoning, trapping, beating, and burning monkeys. By comparison my old professor's strategy seemed quite mild.

'I bought some crackers,' he said. 'To make a bang, you know.'

9.

It was no longer raining, but the morning was misty and when we drove up to Blackridge the hill itself was still hidden in cloud. Mary had the key for the little church, so we all went in to have a look before she left for work at the Diocesan Archive.

It was a place of worship that many of the local residents had helped to build: the Church of the Annunciation of the Blessed Virgin Mary, inaugurated in 1911. Within nine years, when the Smallie family came to live in the neighbourhood with their five children, St Mary's had become a vital node in the small community. It was situated at the centre of things, just below the railway bridge, and a little way from the station. A hundred years later, the house of God looked worn, but durable. I'd liked the curious idea I had from Francois that it was made of cardboard, the paper church. But a bit of research revealed that this story was a confusion that had to do with the malthoid that was used to coat the wooden walls, and had begun over the years to crinkle like paper. Inside, the wood panelling and polished pews gleamed. At the entrance stood a neat pile of hymn books, and at the front an arrangement of fresh flowers. Parishioners had made embroidered cross-stitch kneelers for the pews, and the morning sun through the windows lit up our own Mary's white hair like a revelation.

Above the simple altar, the words 'I am the True Vine,' were carved in dark wood. It was a luscious metaphor of God's viticulture imported from a distant land of miracles and olive trees, but the abundance it called to mind contrasted with the austerity of its representation. I'd recently visited the little church in Taos Pueblo, where images of the Virgin and of Christ are surrounded by bright paintings of maize and squash and beans. But this was Blackridge, after all, not New Mexico. The congrega-

89

tion who built St Mary's were not Catholic. They were not the colonised, nor the subjects of missionary instruction. And they did not have about them the remnants of an animist spirituality. Instead, the rather plain little chapel of the Church of England was a local incarnation of something those early colonials knew well and must have been keen to preserve: a trace of the home they'd left behind, and a taste of the Home that lay beyond; the comforts of faith, music, devotion, community, and ancient ritual; and perhaps a weekly source of shared conviction that made it easier to execute the conquest of the region without too much remorse.

I was glad to visit, but it was not what I was looking for. While my grandmother had played the organ on Sundays, the rest of the family had not been particularly devout. My grandfather was, as my mother put it, frankly uninterested. The elder siblings seemed simply to have done their own thing, and Betty walked out of Sunday school as a small girl.

So the Blackridge church was really the site of what my mother had left behind. Not that she abandoned God, who was in everyone and everything. Just church, at least for a while. Like her father, for the rest of her life she couldn't bear dogma or religious exclusivism. It was an attitude she communicated to me from early on, and shared with the children she taught, so that one memorable year she produced a performance at our Methodist primary school called *Where is the Light?* I remember her working on the script at night, a compilation of poems we'd all written about the quest for Light in different religions. She made sure that every child in the school had a part.

A lifetime later, when my father was hit by a speeding car driven by a paraplegic man without a licence, she began attending a particular parish of the Anglican church in Cape Town known for its good music and lavish rituals. Still, her participation was always on her own terms. Once when a friend from the congregation asked her to be godmother for his new baby, she explained to him that she simply couldn't do it, saying (as she told me afterwards), 'You see, I just don't believe all that stuff.' Yet when her friend Father Lyle suggested she make some vestments, she responded with a fabulous collection of stoles and chasubles, embroidered and appliquéed with bright leaves, birds, stars, flames, flowers, and phoenixes, in silks and gold that would have been at home in Taos or Santa Fe.

I like to imagine there was something of the Blackridge environment in the joy of that embroidery. Now as she lay in the nursing home with dry stiff legs tethered to the blue surgical cushion, the memory of her Sunday morning walks as a child was so vivid that her feet still trod a path through supple grasses. She would talk about the feel of the long grass brushing against your legs, the delicious crunch of burnt stems underfoot, and the new green shoots coming up through the black. The veld was full of birds and insects, gladioli and watsonias in the spring, fire lilies after a winter burn, a porcupine quill on the path, tracks of a little buck. The smell of it was good, the sky was big and good, and walking on the hill on Sunday mornings with Barts or Dad was something completely good.

It was a type of vegetation she would love for the rest of her life, a specific ecosystem in KwaZulu-Natal, now critically endangered, that biologists call the Mistbelt Grassland. I had read that the characteristic Mistbelt pattern – of grasses on the hills and forest patches in the kloofs and along streams – makes for a complex mesh of life that co-evolved with herbivores over millions of years, and is renewed by fire. Nobody knows the particular story of the Blackridge hill, but once human people appeared in the world, grasslands like it were the ground of their being. The rich veld was a place to gather complex carbohydrates – the tubers, bulbs, corms, and roots that were our staple food for most of evolution – and also to hunt, following the animals. More recently, people would move domestic cattle through, setting fire to the grasslands to produce early grazing. As I listened to her stories of Blackridge, I realised that for my mother the experience of that primal ecosystem became, as other memories faded, a quintessential emblem of the beautiful.

After all, it was something human beings have always known: walking on the hill with another person, the movement of wind in long grass, the scratch of seed-heads against your legs, the flash of a bright flower in your path, the possibility of snakes. By the time the family lived there in the 1920s, the railway line, the church, and the surveyor general's maps had largely organised the community of beings that lived below the Ridge into some version of modernity. But it was still possible to wander off on a Sunday morning and walk for hours among the myriad grasses. Red grass, rooigras, *insinde*. The leaves blueish-green and turning to red, and the flowers a distinctive clutch of spikelets on a long stem. Beloved of cows, good grazing.

By the time we left St Mary's that morning to explore the neighbourhood, the mist over the Ridge had dissipated. Colin suggested we drive up the hill to have a look, so we all squeezed into his car and took the road over the old railway bridge. There were a few houses above the line and, beyond them, the hill itself. It was divided into sections, some bare red earth, some dark green plantation. The territory felt inhospitable to further exploration, but one thing seemed clear: the remnant grassland had been erased.

In its place was a stubble of felled tree trunks, and beside them an army of juveniles planted in a neat grid. The hill felt empty, too quiet and still, but the sound of its destruction must have been immense. Like so many other hills in KwaZulu-Natal, the Ridge was now inhabited by the planted grid of a single water-thirsty species of exotic tree whose roots secrete a chemical that kills off local plants because they have no resistance to it, and reduces soil diversity. From the road to the horizon, the land had been occupied by regiments of eucalyptus.

Later, when I called the man from Forestry, he explained that the trees were all clones, replicas of a single original. His friendly enthusiasm for the project of industrial monoculture reminded me of my grandfather's cheerful involvement in the extermination of locusts. From the plantation on the Ridge to everywhere else, the pulp, the woodchips, and the mining timbers traversed the highways of the world, spoils of yet another war.[35]

10.

Then again, things are never what you expect.

We drove back to the old railway servitude to find a small herd of Nguni cattle grazing in the wide green corridor where the train used to travel between the gold mines and the sea. They had great horns and calm faces, and were munching the wild flowers and the long green grass. Their bodies were white and specked with black. Dark red speckles on creamy velvet hide. The cows must have come from Vulindlela on the other side of the ridge. *Izinkomo.* Slow ruminants. How many generations? Although no Iron Age sites have been excavated at Blackridge, I knew that not far away at the Botanical Garden a scattering of pottery shards had been collected at the river, the leavings of a homestead.

Cattle people. Cattle who are people. When did you return? Perhaps you never really left.

We parked the car and joined the cows meandering through the summer green, peering into the forest of high trees and great creepers below the grassy corridor of the railway servitude, taking what paths we could into the deep liveliness of the place. Perhaps before the line was rerouted, someone had built a house there. Perhaps it was my mother's house. At night when I was a child, she used to tell me about lichen and moss. She would talk about the sound of bamboo canes in the wind. And the bush babies, how their eyes gleamed in the dark, and they cried in the trees like real babies.

'Granny lived in paradise,' Sophie said. 'Let's call her and say we're here.'

The sun was high, and the air was full of birdsong. A hawk appeared, circling overhead.

When my mother answered the phone, she said, 'We took it for granted, you know. It was so absolutely wonderful, the feeling of the grounds.'

Then she asked, without all that much concern, 'And did you find the house?'

'Not yet. It may have been demolished, but we're still looking. And we *are* here at Blackridge. The trees are huge, lots of birds.'

'Oh yes . . . I'm so glad you're there. It's a glorious place, isn't it?'

'It's wonderful.'

'And now you've touched that earth, left your footprints there.'

I told her about the hawk overhead, and she said, 'Yes. There was always a hawk.'

'And you know what? We saw a monkey near where the railway line used to be.'

'A monkey! I never said a monkey could come there!' She sounded delighted.

'They're all over Maritzburg now.'

'My goodness.' Once again I could hear her smiling. 'Well there was never a monkey there before.'

A few moments later, my phone rang. It was one of the nurses calling from her room. She wanted to speak to me again.

'Now listen,' she said. 'I've been thinking. I want you to buy some lovely material and make yourself a skirt. From me. You use my money, see? A lovely skirt. Will you do that?'

'Thank you, that sounds wonderful. When I get back.'

'Promise?'

'Yes.'

11.

Over the next few days, equipped with survey drawings and satellite pictures, we checked out every road and watercourse in Blackridge, looking for a wood-and-iron house, or a mango tree, or a stream. It was what they call a quiet neighbourhood: big properties roosting on either side of the green space that was once a railway line, massive trees over-run with honeysuckle, deep hedges of azalea, entire worlds of fern, banana groves inhabited by sleeping bats, the lush Mistbelt forest fed by summer rains and corralled into gardens with lawns and lemon trees, or gone wild again in the unkempt spaces of forgotten dreams, fierce dogs barking behind fences, humans giving birth and dying, birds and mon-keys passing through. My mother had a stream, that at least I knew.

It was in retrospect a curiously trusting – you could say naïve – way to conduct a quest. It was as though, having once left her bedside with a task to accomplish, the fierce power of her imagination was such that I felt sure the vanished garden was still there, and that I'd recognise it if only I knew how to look. It had to be present somewhere. Just hidden in plain sight.

But the time of our visit was running out, my family's patience was pretty much exhausted, and we had found no trace at all of the original house. I felt sad, but unrelenting. It was time to change track completely, I told the others. Check out the deep past.

So on our last morning in Pietermaritzburg I met the archaeologist Gavin Whitelaw in the back rooms of the KwaZulu-Natal Museum, while Michael took the twins to look at the exhibits of stuffed animals. I'd asked Gavin to show me things made by people who lived in the region very long ago, and he selected some artefacts from shelves of neatly labelled cardboard boxes.

We stood there together, and I held them in my hands: ceramic fragments of pots made by farmers, Early Iron Age. Fine stone tools made by hunter-gatherers, Later Stone Age. The classic almond form of a hand-axe made by human beings whose lives we can only imagine, Early Stone Age.

The ancient things were wordless, as they always are. Together they witnessed to the continuity of the craft, as well as to the particular lives of countless humans who knew the neighbourhood of my mother's home, and mine, as their own. The ceramic shards were pieces of a vessel formed by the warm hands of someone who once lived near the river at the place which became what people like my ancestors laid out as the Botanical Gardens, and where, on Sunday afternoons a century later, people like my family would go to feed the ducks, and watch the men in kilts playing bagpipes in an avenue of plane trees. The recent stone tools from Umlaas Road were a reminder that it was there, in a dry watercourse overgrown with thorn trees, that my cousin Ian Smallie, son of my mother's brother Barts, once took her and me to find stone tools. Flints, as we called them then. And the big hand-axe looked just like the multitude of hand-axes that people had made over a period of a million years, all the way from Cape Town to Kathu to East Timor. But this one was excavated a block away from the suburban house where I grew up, near the Foxhill Spruit, that stream where we were forbidden to play for fear of bilharzia.

'Some people get others to do their drawings,' Gavin said, when he showed me his drawings of ceramic shards, 'But. . . if you don't *draw* them, you don't really see them.'

'It makes you look.'

'Yes.'

Then he took me to the pots. They were great wide-bellied earthenware pots, carefully reconstructed from a heap of broken shards. Msuluzi, Ndondondwane, Ntshekane: the names archaeologists give to what they categorise as the three phases of the Early Iron Age. Each time, a living person dug clay out of the ground, formed it into a vessel, burnished it, marked it with fine patterns of parallel lines, triangles, or crosshatchings around the neck, and fired it. Much later, someone else came and gathered up what fragments that they could find. Tried to mend it.

'It's not just that something's been lost. It's that it's been broken. Smashed.'

It was my friend, the historian John Wright, warning me a few weeks before about being what he called 'Romantic'. He was talking about the history of KwaZulu-Natal, but at the time it could just as well have been my mother's memory that he had in mind.

She had used the same word to describe it to me: 'I feel like an egg that's been smashed.'

It was quiet in the museum. The artefacts were silent.

Yet holding them in my hands, their pitiless silence brought into the space of the storeroom an unimaginably long narrative of displacement and continuity in which the brief story of my own family became a single utterance, audible for only a breath.

In that moment, the urgency of my particular quest became a tiny impulse in the long, long reach of human habitation of the region: human beings who make things with their hands, people who live near water. In every generation, there had to be water. A river, a watercourse, a stream.

Back at the Gardners' for lunch, I felt somehow released from obligation, like a child again. The deep past can do that to you. Bring you back.

Next day, we'd be leaving, and I wanted to see Blackridge one last time. There was the promise to find something growing for my mother. But more than that I wanted simply to be quiet.

'I'd just like to go up there again,' I explained to Colin. 'Forget about looking for the house, just walk a bit and sit still. I want to "just be", as my mother used to say.'

'If that's what you need to do, then do it,' he said gravely. 'I'll stay at home with the twins. Assuming they don't want to sit and listen to the tiny voices of insects.'

They did not.

Michael and I walked along the lush green railway servitude to the low brick wall of the station platform. The place where Betty would have stood waiting for the train on school mornings was overgrown with grasses and flowers, the railway track itself gone to green, a long reach of meadow grazed by the chief's cows. Along the base of the wall a little moisture had collected, as it does at the edge of a big rock in the veld, and ferns were growing in a crack between the bricks. Probably it was illegal simply to dig them out. They were indigenous plants, after all, and I had no collector's permit. But I felt a certain right to take them home for her, and I knew that nobody else would care.

Digging, sweating, barefoot. Walking in the grass, toes in the wet after the previous day's rain, you enter a realm of yellow dandelions, black-eyed Susans, a tough old rose, purple verbenas. The afternoon is alive with cicadas and many birds, voices of midsummer. Dig up a maiden-hair fern from the edge of the abandoned railway, track of the big black locomotive gone to cows and grasses. Make it two ferns. Was it an act of nostalgia? Transgression? Frances Cope carried acorns to the Natal Midlands in the 1870s, and her book is full of the plants Koppie finds in the veld and coaxes to grow. Botanising, she calls it. My paternal grandfather did it too, with his hatred of syringas and a special love of the indigenous cabbage tree.

Digging up, transplanting, naming. This thing we do. Betty and Cyril made mud pies from this earth, baked them under this sun. A trace, a thread: keep it safe, bring it home, something growing.

Afterwards I meandered for a while or sat alone and quite still, listening. Among the myriad voices of the afternoon was the call of the particular dove who used to begin the children's programme on Radio Bantu in the 1960s: '*Amdokwe, amdokwe, amabele, avuthiwe ehlanzeni!*' It was an insistent voice full of summer, a message from my own suburban childhood in which the dove appears to remind the human people that the *mabele* is ripe.

In my mother's memory, the same doves at Blackridge spoke English, and their call was about family: 'Bob's father! Bob's father! Bob's father!' she told me.

'Everyone was together then,' she went on, looking back across the years of broken shards.

Perhaps my hopeful quest had been to repair things, like the people in the museum storeroom who draw pictures, make inventories, and try their best to glue together the fragments. But my mother's state of mind could never be mended, and now even her vanished home was irretrievable: that place where everyone is together, a place of remembering, a place to remember you.

Yet for a brief unmeasurable while that afternoon, deep in her grasses and flowers, butterflies and cicadas filling the air, hawk circling overhead, feet in her mud, I knew with utter clarity the place I was looking for. In the multitude of grasses where the railway used to be, this living world is no memory. This love of leaf and creatures is something ineradicable: gift of a small girl playing in the world.

12.

We left early for the long trip home, two days. Driving back, the big roads were clogged with big trucks carrying big cargo. If the railway was once the major artery of carbon through the land, this double-carriage highway had now replaced it as the neural net of the global mind.

Imagine a world without Rainbow Chickens, the sign read. Imagine a world in which the big wide roads lead straight to your destination without ever meandering into byways. Imagine a story that powers through a life like this unrelenting national road.

At dusk, we reached Colesberg, and climbed stiffly out of the car to a twittering and a scuffling from the high eucalyptus trees. And then we saw them: great clouds of birds in the changing light, reddish bodies swooping and gathering, and coming down to roost in the branches, a wonder of multitudes.

Kestrels, someone said. The migratory Lesser Kestrel. Each year, during December and January, they arrive from the north in great flocks, travelling the old sky paths across the earth. Imagine a world without them.

THE DARK

1.

'I missed you,' my mother said when I called her.

'Yes. But I did phone quite often.'

'Julie, my brain has defeated me. I'll just have to live from hour to hour.'

Our house-sitters had told us about her calls. How she'd explain, sometimes several times a day, that she was Julia's sister, and that they were to let me know that she was coming home.

Later when we visited, she said again, 'My brain is gone.'

'Okay, I'll test you,' Sky said. 'What's this one's name?'

She took on the task like the miller's daughter answering Rumpelstiltskin on the third day.

'Jane ... Jacoba ... Julia!'

'And this one?'

'Diana ... Petrolia ... Sophie!'

'And me?'

'John ... Jacobus ... Sky!'

We all laughed. Next, he said he'd do a sums quiz.

'Oh,' she said, looking concerned, 'I was very, very, *very* terrible at arithmetic.'

But his instinct was correct. He tested her with a heap of mental arithmetic sums, each more difficult than the last. She got them all right.

'Oh, I feel years younger!' she said afterwards. 'It's given me quite a lift.'

About Blackridge, she was unconcerned that we hadn't found the actual site, but over the next while it became clear that our going there had opened something up. Whenever I asked her about specific places and people — still hoping, perhaps, to construct a map of home — she would respond to the question at another level, unearthing buried

103

regions she'd never mentioned before: the hidden place under the wood-and-iron house, and the dark room at the centre.

'There's a Simpson Road,' I said. 'I wonder if it was nearby.'

'Oh yes, there were Simpsons. An important family. They lived near the church . . .'

And then she continued, smiling, 'I can feel myself *now* crawling under the house and keeping a good eye for snakes. I played there a lot with Cyril.'

This was the first time she had mentioned the place under the house, but it now became something she returned to often.

'We saw what was probably the stationmaster's house,' I told her. 'Do you remember that?'

'The Johnsons lived above, at the end. I think they had a shop. The daughter must have been very intelligent. She was a civil servant, very high up, and she wrote something about the City Hall . . . And there was Uplands School too. The school Mother went to. It was *the* school.'

'And the Ridge itself? What was it like? Do you know why it was called Blackridge?'

'Perhaps there were fires at one time. When we lived there, there were just grasses growing there. It was lovely. Barts used to take me up there on a Sunday, and he used to sing.'

The conversation meandered on. Then I asked her about animals, and heard for the first time ever the story of Marcus and the dark room.

'Alsatians,' she said. 'Old Marcus, the father of the whole lot. In the middle of the house was what we called the dark room. It had no outlet except the door. That was a thing of those houses.'

I tried to imagine it. A room without windows. A room without windows at the centre of the house. How could anyone possibly choose to design such a place? Having grown up with a beloved father whose periodic depressions kept him lying for weeks in a darkened bedroom, I'd spent the rest of my life opening curtains.

'Anyway,' she continued, 'Jock was the dog man, and he had these lovely Alsatians. I particularly liked Marcus, and he seemed to recognise me. And *one* day, I went inside and I couldn't find him. The house had the dark room, you know. It was central. I looked for Marcus everywhere, and I couldn't find him. Then I went into the dark room to find something else. He lifted up his head to lick my hand. I stroked him and stroked him and stroked him till he couldn't hold his head up anymore. Then that was it. There was a thud. I was so sad when he died. I felt at the time that he waited for me. He was pitch black. His mate's name was Sally. We had that couple, and their pups.'

We were all quiet.

After a while, someone asked about cats.

'Yes,' she said vaguely, 'there were cats, but not of much social importance . . . We were told never to play under the house, and of course we immediately played under the house . . . The train journeys I didn't enjoy. They were very close-knit people on the trains. They all knew each other. I was regarded as a very dull person. I was prim. Very prim. Oh God.'

'Which means what, exactly?'

'Afraid of sex. That is the only way I can put it. If there was a girl who had a boyfriend, that was a girl you didn't talk to.'

'Do you think that primness came from your mother?'

'Ja. It was unspoken, but very much in the air. Some people had a shop on the hill. The eldest girl . . . we were very shocked because she wore *silk stockings*!'

'Why was that so shocking?'

'It meant she was cheap. Other people wore black stockings. She must have spent a lot on clothes. Those things were so important in such a tiny settlement . . . And Julie used to look after a child, the doctor's child, and the child used to come and play sometimes. This girl said something about the male and female dogs. I wish I could remember . . . But there was something in the air, and poor Doodie was saying, "Oh no! Don't talk about that . . . It's very rude!" That was typical of the time. And you know, a big family developed out of all that.'

Like a small child who shifts quickly and unselfconsciously from one mood to the next, the flow of her memories wandered from image to image without check. The place under the house. The dark room at the centre. The pair of silk stockings.

'You would have loved my father,' she said. 'And I remember his parents. She was a cross old bastard, and he was very, very old and he would sit apart from everyone.'

'Did you try and talk to him?'

'No! Shh!' She put on a fierce face. 'Grandparents have such a chance, you know, if they only thought about it. A chance of character-building, of making things happy. Barts used to sing to me.'

'Like you and the twins.'

'Well, it's just like the changing of people's hair: getting old. It happens. It's part of the infinite life of reality. I think about that much more these days. I think about the vast, vast, *vast* reality.'

'And how do you think you turned out as you did?'

'I don't know. School does it to you, I think. I went to Longmarket Street first, and I *hated* those trips in the train. The boys were horrible to me. It was quite a long way to get me to the station every day. It was a long distance when you didn't have a car.'

I told her about the grasses now growing on the station platform. Said we'd dug up some ferns and brought them back.

'I'll put them in plant pots for you, and bring them around when they're established. And some photographs.'

She looked completely happy.

'Oh, you've turned up the soil!' she said. 'Under the surface, made me look at it under the surface! You've woken me up inside. Thank you very much!'

'Our going to Blackridge has stirred things up.'

'You've stirred me up like boiling porridge!'

2.

'How is Mother?' she would ask, nearly every time. And when I hesitated, 'Has Mother died? Why didn't you tell me?'

Mother, Mother, Mother. Was this after all what I was looking for? In every story of Blackridge, my grandmother was both present and distinctly absent. And as the quest began to wander into the darker spaces of the house, I realised I had to find out more about the person she called Mother, my grandmother Madge Tatham who died before I was born. Her daughter Betty had lived a long and creative life without much reference to her, but dementia, as they call it, breaks things apart and muddles them up. Like an egg that's been smashed. And it takes you back to the beginning. Whatever Blackridge meant, the person she called Mother had to be part of it.

'Your mother didn't write a diary, or keep letters, did she?'

'No!' She was quite emphatic, taking on a stern voice not quite her own. 'Oh, don't be silly.'

'How do you mean, silly?'

'You're not to talk about yourself at all!'

She was speaking in the present tense about a time nearly ninety years ago.

'Because it's vain?' Sophie was sitting beside her.

'To talk about yourself is vanity,' she explained. 'The great thing was to try and pretend you weren't there. The great thing was to wash the dishes. You had to pretend that you were not about, but you *did* wash the dishes. That was my mother.'

It was midday in the nursing home. She was lying in bed, eating the chocolate éclair we'd brought. It was a messy, delicious confection, certain to displace lunch.

'Worst of all was to be a nuisance,' she continued. 'You were allowed to wash the dishes, but you were not to make people notice you. You were not supposed to be about. You were not supposed to be *anybody*. In other words, you were not to show off.'

'Did you show off?'

'Yes, me especially.'

'By doing what?'

'Opening your mouth. She was very good at making you shut it. She looked at you with a *hard* look. Then you were quiet.'

'What if you didn't?'

'I don't think that ever happened.'

'And how did you manage to be so different from all that? You were always your own person.'

It was one of the questions that remained with me. How had she escaped?

'I suppose you just found a way out.' She was looking at the syringa tree through the sliding glass door. 'You know, like a little squirrel, trying this branch and then that branch . . . But, yes, you did get out of it. With some difficulty.'

'Why do you think she became like that?'

'Well her father was the chief man in Dundee, the mayor. That was quite something. We were a disappointment. I was brought up to think I was a disappointment. I was very fond of her because she was my mother, but there was not much affection.'

'And what would she do on your birthday?' Sophie wanted to know.

'Nothing special. I can remember a table outside and a birthday cake. You weren't to eat too much. Letty became my special person. She was ten years older. So when I had a birthday she made sure I had a good birthday. And she looked after my clothes. She would buy presents for me, and she'd make sure I had a pretty dress. Mother was . . . too busy.'

We were quiet for a bit.

Then she said, 'Oh poor Mother. I shouldn't give her such a bad picture. Take away fifty per cent of what I've said. Her own mother died when she was very little. She *adored* her father.'

'But she didn't show her feelings much,' Sophie said.

'No! That was a cheap thing to do.'

For all my searching, the Blackridge house had remained hidden. But my grandmother Madge simply would not stay dead.

3.

I gathered together the small collection of things we had from her, Mary Madeline Smallie, née Tatham. Madge.

By comparison with my grandfather's hundreds of pages of letters and reflections, it was a sparse archive. She had left behind no thoughts on either public or private life. No records of war or work or disaster or journeys across the world. No stories of home or love or apprehension. Not even songs. Instead, from this most unrelenting ancestor my mother had inherited some photographs, a large ostrich-feather fan with tortoise-shell fittings, a Hungarian black silk jacket embroidered with bright flowers, a silver-plated fruit bowl held aloft in the chubby arms of a little boy whose left foot rested on a snail, a big brass saucepan for making jam, a single novel, and two recipe books.

To imagine the environment in which Madge lived as a young girl, the life to which she was accustomed, I had to read backwards through another story of devastation.

In my grandfather's suitcase of papers was a report written in the year she turned seventeen by the town clerk of Dundee and signed by Madge's father, WH Tatham. Its purpose was to record the state of the town as they found it on the seventeenth of May 1900 in the wake of the Boer occupation during the first months of the South African War. The document is an account of the destruction wrought by the enemy. But in its meticulous attention to shattered detail, it calls up a ghostly image of the world of material things in which my grandmother had been raised, and which her family took as their due.

At Mr Tatham's house, the town clerk writes, horses and cattle had been stabled in the rooms, the floors torn up, furniture smashed, and there was broken crockery and glassware all over the floor. Even the stoves, he notes, were broken. At his own house, the garden which was usually bright with flowers was trampled, fruit trees torn down, and all the furniture cleared out except for a handsome roll-top desk that had been smashed because it was too heavy to move. The Masonic Hall was filled with a great stack of sideboards, sofas, washstands, smashed mirrors, and destroyed oil paintings, all heaped together with eighteen pianos. Elsewhere they found a large assortment of watchmaker's machinery and tools, thirty or forty clocks, packets of watch glasses and springs, all mixed up in a most extraordinary manner, he said, with crockery, carpentry tools, and books. All the grandfather clocks in the town were smashed underfoot. The banks and the chemist's shop had been looted, the wagon maker's shop set on fire, both churches vandalised, and the printer's trays capsized so that all the type lay about in heaps. In the Dundee Coalfields area, the report records that the mineshafts, the engines, and boilers were blown to pieces, and in Mr Tatham's offices the strongroom and safes had been broken open and papers strewn about so that everything that at other times presented a picture of order and neatness resembled, as he puts it, a veritable pigsty.

The town clerk has no language by which to imagine a motivation for this astonishing rage of mayhem. His report is formal, but he is clearly in shock. The word to which he keeps returning is 'smashed.'[36]

That morning the young mining town was in ruins. But within a couple of years, Dundee shook off the impact of its destruction to become a booming centre of colonial industry and culture. It was not long before Sunnyside, as my Tatham ancestors' house was optimistically named, was restored to a state of gracious gentility. And soon it was further renovated to exceed even the high levels of comfort that Madge and her family had known before the War. When her widowed father remarried, and his English wife required a double storey, he simply commissioned a second one to be built on top of the first, so that the new mansion – one of the first in the country to be fitted with electricity as well as piped water – boasted four large reception rooms, six vast bedrooms, a bathroom, a kitchen, a larder, a butler's pantry, a washhouse, extensive stables, a carriage house and a cowshed.[37] If this were a fairy tale, it would by now be apparent that my great-grandfather, whose business was in law and property transactions, had overreached himself. But the crash when it came was still some years away.

Meanwhile, on the darker side of town, the men who mined the coal from the black seam underground that fuelled this dream of civilisation continued to live in filthy, overcrowded rooms. The walls had not been whitewashed for years. There was nowhere to do your laundry. Human shit lay in the gutters. And the Dundee Coal Company considered the provision of beds or bunks to be an unnecessary expense that would disturb the shareholders. As a consequence, many people got sick. Many of them died. Their families received scant compensation. For while the rituals of colonial Dundee society had been swiftly reconstructed after the barbarian occupation, the barbaric condition of daily devastation in the compounds was deemed too costly to repair.[38]

4.

In August 1903, Madge was twenty years old when she inscribed her name on the opening page of *Hilda's "Where Is It?" Of Recipes: Containing Amongst Other Practical And Tried Recipes Many Old Cape, Indian, And Malay Dishes And Preserves: Directions for Polishing Furniture, Cleaning Silk, etc, And A Collection of Home Remedies in Case of Sickness.* It was a gesture that marked the first step towards another life. The War was over, and she was engaged to be married in just under a year.

The family stories depict her as a tall young woman, stylishly dressed, who played the violin and the piano quite beautifully. Her mother had died when she was very young, and the pain of it was never spoken of. But as long as she was living at Sunnyside under the protection of her beloved father, such comfort as wealth can provide must have seemed assured, and poor people a distant shadow in the neighbourhood.

For what could Miss Tatham know of the real cost of coal, the ongoing horrors of the mine, the ruthlessness of electric lights? She faced the world with dark eyes and a firm mouth, and where others in a group photograph might move or fidget during the long exposure, her gaze is steady and unblurred, her bearing upright. Or rather, as my mother wrote with characteristic irony on the back of one such picture, 'stately'. In that particular scene, Madge commands the centre of an extended family group assembled outside the Dundee mansion. She is wearing a fine lace bodice nipped in at the waist, a long skirt elegantly adorned with brocade, and a magnificent black hat. To her right, WH Tatham sits at ease, the distinguished mayor among unidentified elderly relatives.

Most of the party engage the camera with an air of relaxed superiority. They were, after all, a white aristocracy in a fast-expanding town where rich coal deposits, exploitable black labour, and the enterprising industry of the mining company were making many things possible for people of their class. Ascendant again after the Boer occupation, cultured citizens like my ancestors had reason to feel comfortable. But at the edge of the group is a man leaning in towards the camera with his weight on one leg. He is dressed in an ill-fitting black suit, and his features are strained.

'Oh, he doesn't like it, does he?' my mother said.

We were gathered around her bed, as usual, and she was pointing to the person who would become my grandfather, Madge's young fiancé Major Alan Smallie, whose love would carry her away to a succession of different houses, almost a different world.

'It was her hair that did it, you know,' she went on. 'He told me once that he saw her standing under a green tree with the light in her long dark hair.'

Beautiful Madge had grown up with plenty of servants. So leaving home with Alan to become mistress of her own house meant she would need a great deal of practical information about the correct way of doing things. Without a mother to instruct her, *Hilda's "Where Is It?"* must have seemed invaluable.

The book is no match for Mrs Beeton, but it does offer a detailed job description for a bride-to-be in her circumstances. In the Introduction, Hildagonda Duckitt, who lived on the family farm near Darling with an oven that could bake seventy loaves of bread at a time, writes warmly to her readership both at home and abroad as though they were her friends. Offered as a conversation between the Cape and England, the collection is distinctly, self-consciously, colonial.

Much of what Madge was to learn from Hilda comfortingly affirmed the staples of a familiar way of life. There are recipes for Potatoes (How to Boil), Porridge (For Breakfast), Bread (Brown), Beef Steak (Broiled), Cold Meat (To Do Up), Eggs (Poached), and Fish (Fried). Whether in Australia or Canada or elsewhere in Africa, to be a British colonial housewife at the turn of the century you not only had to know how to keep furniture and floors polished and glassware sparkling, but also how to cook a variety of animals, to steam puddings, to make certain sweet cakes and scones for afternoon tea, and to put up bottles of jams and preserves.

It was a starchy, meaty cuisine, full of sugar, eggs, and butter, with very little mention of vegetables, and its impact reached across the planet. To put English food on the dinner table, a great community of animals must continually be raised, nurtured, and killed. Numerous lively and diverse local ecosystems had to be destroyed and irrevocably reconstructed for the industrial production of sugar and wheat. An immense imperial network of ships and seafaring commerce had to be maintained to procure tea, spices, and other essentials from all over the Empire. And a great traffic of labouring human beings must be transported far and forever from their own homes to produce and service this master diet. But stories of trade, industry, and global markets were not Hilda's concern. Her task was to tell you, the female reader, and the 14 000 others who owned the book by the time of Madge's 1902 edition, how to master the culinary rituals of your kind.

She could also pass on more exotic food wisdom from the Cape. There is Mrs Rose-Innes's recipe for bottled fruit, Mrs Van der Riet's Walnut Tart, and even Admiral Etheridge's recipe for Ginger Pop. From Hilda, Madge could learn about Mebos, Biltong (which people suffering from *mal de mer* on board ship have relished when no other delicacy would tempt them to eat), Bredee, Moss Bolletjes (an old Dutch Recipe from Mrs Moorries. Very Good), Vanderhum (10 bottles of brandy, 50 cloves, 20 tablespoonsful of finely-cut Naartjepeel), Sasaties, Koesisters (a Batavian sweetmeat. Will keep for months), Poffertjes . . . And she could even find out how to improvise an oven from an antheap in the veld, or mince up the fat from an indigenous fat-tailed sheep.

Such recipes gave a different take on Dutch settler culture from what my young grandmother had probably been led to believe about the enemy after the occupation of Dundee. In Hilda's book, there is no Boer War. Instead, in recipe after recipe, things Dutch are delicious (foods seasoned with long years of repetition, matured in the warm kitchens of old homesteads, fragrant with orchards), and old Cape families love nutmeg and green fig preserve, and could even teach an English housewife how to improve a pot of tea with orange blossoms.

And then there is the Indian food. Once at the nursing home when

I asked my mother what meals she remembered from Blackridge, all she could think of was curry. This probably said more about her memory than about the family menu. But certainly, by the early twentieth century, British cooking had about a hundred and fifty years of familiarity with the imperial construct they called curry, and one of the kitchen basics was what they called 'curry powder'.[39] In contrast with this sort of appropriation, Hilda's recipes are (she assures the reader) especially authentic. Her Mutton Curry is made as taught to her by an Indian cook, and the recipe for Bengal Chutney was sourced from an English lady who had long resided in India.

Holding Hilda's "Where Is It?" in my hands, I wonder how Madge used the book. Did she ever read recipes as a form of fantasy? Of course not, my mother would say. No time, no money, too many children. But perhaps it was not always so. Perhaps even Mrs Smallie sometimes dreamt of Almond Cake (500 almonds pounded in rose water, 12 eggs, a pound of sugar . . .) or imagined the possibility of Scalloped Oysters. Whatever else, she marked her copy well with notes and food stains, and it must have helped to give her competence and courage as she took charge of the successive households that she, the mayor of Dundee's beautiful daughter, came to share in difficult circumstances with the man her family called a dreamer.

A few months after they were married, she wrote a recipe for Yeast on one of the blank pages. Over time she added instructions for other household preparations. As my mother explained, my grandmother thought it cheap to show your feelings, or to talk about yourself. But a century later, in the absence of other testimonies written in her lively hand, the bare instructions for basic domestic products offer a small window through which to peer into her life.

This is what she wrote about: Starch for Collars and Shirts, Eno's Fruit Salts, Extract of Malt and Cod Liver Oil, a remedy for Rough Red Arms.

5.

There was a kind of relief in having relinquished the search for the actual house. I planted the ferns in terracotta pots and the little oak sapling in the ground. I followed my mother's meanderings, wherever they led. And I read Madge's recipe books.

But not long after I began excavating stories of my grandmother, an email appeared from Colin Gardner.

He wrote, 'I have had a telephone answering machine message from Audrey Tanner, who says that you know her (or know of her?) and have her telephone number. She thinks she has some more information about what she called "the old house in Thorpe Lane". Were we sure that the house you are looking for is in Thorpe Lane? Anyhow, I'm sure you'll give her a ring. It would be a great pity if it turns out that the house is there all the time and we missed it.'

Ah well. I didn't in fact know Audrey, but someone had suggested I get in touch with her when we'd visited. What could I do now but call her? I wanted to.

'You know, when you phoned from Blackridge the other night, I wasn't thinking straight. A bit taken aback.' Her voice, with its particular regional intonation, sounded like the women from my childhood. 'Now it's taken me a while to think clearly about this, but I think I know where the house is.'

'Is? You mean it's still there?'

'I'm almost positive.'

'Tell me about it.'

'It's in Thorpe Lane, between Highfield and Uplands roads. We used to live in Thorpe Lane, and we'd go along to the end of the road, then up a right turn into a pathway towards the railway station, with the waiting room and the other buildings. And the old wood–and–iron house was there, below the railway line. Your mother did say it was below?'

'Yes.'

'And the house has a verandah all around.'

'Yes. And she says it was up off the ground.'

'That's what I was going to say,' she said, 'raised off the ground.'

'The children were told not to play there,' I told her.

'But of course they did.'

'And what happened to the house?'

'Well the Nicholls family lived there, and then Mr and Mrs Lewis, and then Dr Charlton. He built another house in front of it.'

'And the old house?'

'It's still there. The house *is* there.'

Something like a shiver or a shudder passed through me. Uncanny. She was very sure.

'That's amazing.'

Audrey was apologetic: 'I'm sorry I didn't think of it earlier.'

'No problem. You're certain it's still there?'

'I'm positive it's still there.'

'That's incredible.'

'Yes, and you were there all the time.'

'Wow, Audrey,' I said. 'Thank you so much. I'll ask my friend at the surveyor general's office to help me track down the title deeds.'

A few days later, an email came in from Francois.

'Yes,' he told me, 'there *is* a tin house at number 18 Thorpe Lane.'

He'd been for a walk in the neighbourhood and seen the edge of a green tin roof. Back in the office he found that it was built in 1898, and was now owned by someone with the name of G Tegg.

6.

Once the ferns had begun to send out nubs of new growth, the twins and I took them to my mother's room, along with a small branch covered in lichen. She was delighted to see them, wanting the ferns to live on the verandah and the lichen right beside her.

Then we showed her the photos of Blackridge on my laptop. Cattle grazing along the railway servitude. Old brick paths green with moss. High trees overgrown with creepers. She was engrossed.

Looking at the picture of wild banana trees, she said, 'Reminds me of Chagall. That's very Chagall.'

About the railway line itself, abandoned and alive with grasses and wildflowers, she said, 'Oh let it be like that for a long time. Forever!'

And looking at the glade of Mistbelt forest below the railway line, she smiled and remembered.

'The bush babies! You would hear them – waaa waaa – like a baby crying.'

'Where were they?'

'In the bushy part.'

'So there was still some wild bush?'

'*Yes*,' she said emphatically. 'Near the railway line.'

She hadn't mentioned the bush babies since I was a child, but seeing the picture brought them back.

'The bush babies in the trees at night . . .' she went on. 'You could see the little eyes looking at you as you went past.'

The next picture was more tangled forest, and she gasped when she saw it.

'Oh isn't that lovely! Look at all those greens . . . I hope they never spoil it.'

It was the one she kept coming back to, and she asked me to enlarge it and print it out.

'Oh gosh that is absolutely perfect,' she said. 'If the government had any sense at all they would buy it and keep it like that.'

She went on then to tell us about 'all kinds of wild birds'.

'Can you remember what the birds were?'

'No. Just wild birds, wild canaries. Fancy letting a place like that die out.'

'Well it hasn't really died out. It's still there.'

'Yes. That bush is still there. That feeling is still there. Oh I hope they have the sense to keep it. The place was mostly ploughed-up land when we were there. But certainly, some bush too. It was a big mistake, leaving Blackridge.'

I mentioned Mr Gilchrist, how her father had left his job because he felt Mr Gilchrist had been mistreated.

'Oh Gilly,' she smiled. 'He used to tell me about the Bible. The ark and all the different animals. You know, since you've reached some sort of conversation about this, Blackridge has come so alive. Dad in his work-shop making lovely bits of furniture. He used to escape there. He loved it. Everything he made was perfect. He taught at the Tech. And little old Mr Gilchrist, George Gilchrist, a little old man with white hair ... I didn't have ordinary comics or anything, but he used to give me *Christian* magazines. Very dull. I wonder if that old man planted those things in my mind, the doings in the Bible.'

Then somehow she remembered, also for the first time, that the Nicol family used to live next door in a double-storey house.

'On the night David was born, the doctor was drunk. So Dad went and roared for Mrs Nicol to come. I can see him now, climbing through the fence.'

Six-year-old Betty was the youngest child, and the family's awkward silence about people's bodies meant nobody had explained to her that Mother was pregnant. Then all at once one night there she was having a baby in the bedroom, and Dad was running across the garden to fetch Mrs Nicol.

As we looked at more photographs, they dislodged a sort of wistfulness.

'If people could just *be* without remembering or longing,' she said, 'be like cows, that would be good.'

'But animals *do* remember,' Sophie objected.

'Yes, all animals remember. And if you let yourself think about that you get sick from misery. Animals going to the slaughter . . . I won't eat meat. I *can't* eat meat. The cattle were *friends* to us.'

I told her about the monkey we'd seen at Blackridge, and she said, 'Oh what a good idea.'

We sat around her bed, eating biscuits. The twins told her about school and friends, but soon she was back at Blackridge.

Since our visit to KwaZulu-Natal, she had returned again and again to the place under the house. Always it was a realm of thrilling transgression, a dark and secret place that invited the deep mystery which happens when children play, outside of adult supervision. But the dark windowless room at the centre of the house had also returned from the past. And the memories unearthed by our trip brought her back repeatedly to Mother's unrelenting rule, and a child's pain encoded in the death of dogs.

'I can feel *now* the thrill of going underground where we weren't supposed to go,' she told us. 'We were warned that nasty people lived there. And snakes. Snakes were a real problem. The nasty people were imaginary.'

'What did people do if they saw a snake?'

'I don't think anyone ever saw one. It was a sort of myth.'

'We were shocked at the eldest daughter of the people who delivered milk,' she said. 'She wore *silk stockings*! That wasn't nice. I suppose poor Letty would have given anything for a pair of silk stockings. I was just a little girl.'

Then she told us again the story of the shooting. The first time, it was Bindle who was killed. Now it was Ladybird. Same trauma, muddled names.

'One day,' she said, 'remember, Ladybird was an Alsatian. For some reason – I can't remember what the trouble was – Mother made Jock shoot her. I just remember Jock broken-hearted, and I hated my mother for doing it. He took her down to the bush, and he took me with him. I never heard the other side of the story. I never said anything. I just walked next to him.'

'It's so awful,' I said.

'Oh it's excruciating. Looking back on it, that Mother should tell Jock he should shoot her. He was the animal person. I remember that walk . . . Oh God.'

'And then,' she continued with a wry laugh, 'to make matters worse, sometime after that Mother bought an Alsatian. She was a very strong woman. Not very loveable. She didn't have a mother. She didn't know what a mother was.'

'It feels good that we're doing this,' I said.

'Oh, it's lovely for me. And we used to fight so much, you and I.'

'No, that was Doodie. I'm not your sister.'

'Oh! So who are you?'

'Your daughter.'

'Oh yes. Well I wondered why you'd changed! It feels, my brain, like an old thing with holes in it. Things drop through.'

The afternoon was warm and still. Sky fed the pigeons.

My mother said, 'Mrs D will be so furious.'

Sophie played her flute.

'Oh Sophie,' she exclaimed, 'I can feel myself walking over the hills. Did you know you were playing the hills? You must have.'

The next piece was brighter, sparkling.

'It's a song about a blackbird!' she said. 'It's got all my body's nerves going, rattling with it.'

We looked at the pictures of Blackridge again, and she pointed to the big trees.

'Huge. I remember the trees especially. And sometimes you could see a creature.'

'What about the mango tree?'

'It had *great* big leaves.'

I showed her pictures of the contemporary houses.

'Yes, it was a small house,' she said. 'A cottage. It was a plain little wood cottage up on stilts so you could crawl underneath. The garden was huge. That was the thing. And we just took it for granted. Lots of those huge trees.'

Her favourite picture now was one I'd taken on the old railway track: grasses growing through the stones, and at the centre the spikey symmetrical leaves of a wild lettuce, another alien invader.

'Oh I know those little leaves so well!' she exclaimed. 'Look, everything makes a pattern. I like that idea about people too. Everything makes a pattern.'

I pointed out the railway gravels among the green: 'You can still see where the line was. But the wild has taken over.'

'Yes, the wild is lovely. Yes, taking over. I can feel myself jumping across that. That's beautiful. The *patient* patterning . . . I could look at this all day.'

As we were leaving, she pointed to the long branch of the syringa tree: 'That branch. I call it Squirrel Way. Or Squirrel Walk. And I imagine different addresses, like 30 Squirrel Walk, for all the people who lived there.'

'Like who?'

'I don't know. Oh, I suppose the Greens. It's imaginary. Little people living there, 30 Squirrel Walk.'

'And who lived at number 30?

'I don't think I knew the people. And if they wanted to come down from that branch in a hurry, they'd grab a spider web and come down. Sometimes a lichen would get old and crinkle up, and you might easily trip over it.'

Play, play, and pattern. At Blackridge, she learnt how to play.

Later that evening she phoned in a great panic. Said she was shaking, and her voice did sound out of breath.

'I didn't know where you *were!* Oh *please* come and see me!'

She had forgotten the photographs, though she remembered Sophie's flute. We had to go through the same old story about Mother and Dad: who was alive and who was dead. Agonising.

7.

A very strong woman, she called her. Not very loveable. My grand-mother. I had to find out more.

In 1912, Mrs Alan Smallie – for in those days women assumed not only the surname of their husband, but also their Christian name – inscribed the first recipe in a new book of her own. It was for Tapioca Cream and involved boiled tapioca, sugar, whipped cream, and vanilla.

Years later, my mother had the notebook bound in red cloth, and recorded in her neatest handwriting on the inside cover the place where the collection was begun. Harden Heights was a hamlet in the Natal Midlands distinguished for being the site of one of the earliest commer-cial plantations of the black wattle stock that subsequently proliferated to invade the region.

Aside from this date and location, the recipe book gives no hint of the changes that had taken place in my young grandmother's life since her marriage. But her husband's writings make it clear that some things had altered irrevocably.

Once Alan began farming near Dundee, a child was born every two years. Then East Coast fever took hold in the region. It was a plague spread by ticks that ravaged cattle for several years, and catastrophically destroyed what was left of the African homestead economy. When it came to the turn of their farm in 1910, the young couple were helpless against it. Every single one of the cows died.

If the marriage was a pivotal moment for Madge, then that particular year must have been another. She had three small children to feed (four-year-old Clive, two-year-old Letty, and baby Jock) and the farm was lit-tered with dead and dying cows. Then, just when it must have seemed that things could not get worse, her father's business went bankrupt, he lost the great double-storey house in Dundee with all its rooms and electricity, and died of a heart attack at the age of fifty-three.

'Oh yes, Mother adored him,' my mother said, the next time we visited. 'When he died, she had a sort of stroke. He was William Henry, a very rich and well-known man. I don't know if this was true, but it was said that she got a white patch down the side of her neck, a snow-white patch, when he died.'

'Do you remember that patch?' I had never heard of it before.

'Oh yes.'

Alan and Madge had to give up the farm. No alternative. But his experience as an officer in the South African War secured him a job as manager of the New Guelderland Sugar Company, one of the defining projects of the new industrial monoculture that was beginning to occupy parts of the Colony. He was given, as he puts it in the short, handwritten story of his life, full powers over all the estates. According to this account, the work went well enough, but the coastal climate did not agree with the family. So within about a year, having hardly settled into the new house, they moved inland where he was employed as manager and secretary of another institution of enterprise and exploitation, the Harden Heights Wattle Company. A new baby – Florence, whom they called Doodie – was born. And Madge began her recipe collection.

As she shepherded children and belongings from one house to the next across the Colony, she would probably have tried to keep her trousseau linen crisp and clean, and the wedding presents well-polished, our silver-plated fruit bowl, for instance. But the Hungarian black silk jacket embroidered with bright flowers and the ostrich-feather fan must surely by this time have been packed away, along with the other pretty clothes from her Dundee youth. Still, her husband records that he was earning £400 a year, and his position in the company held some status.[40] Perhaps the bare new notebook felt like a fresh start.

Over the next few years the family moved again several times and Madge gave birth to two more children. First was Elizabeth Madeline, named after her mother, but known as Betty. It was 1918, a desperate year when once again my grandfather had no source of income, having resigned from yet another job. Then in 1919 they moved to Blackridge where his new post at the Tech transformed the family's circumstances. And in 1925 David was born.

During all this time, Madge continued to record recipes and the names of the women who had given them to her. The numbered entries are written in black ink in an attractive, confident hand whose meticulous assertion of detail now seems poignant. Such care she took in the listing of ingredients, such precision of method for the transformation of things.

'The food was always correct,' my mother said one day, when I asked what they used to eat.

'Very correct. You didn't eat anything special. Mother was . . . Oh that was a big mistake . . . She was keen to go to church, and Dad thought it was a lot of nonsense.'

Most of my grandmother's recipes were for cakes, puddings, and biscuits. A lifetime later her daughter loved sweet things, but could hardly remember anything delicious that her mother had made.

'What about ice cream?'

Recipe 181 tells how to pack ice or snow, frost or hail, in combination with coarse salt (eight parts ice, one part salt) to freeze several different kinds of ice cream. As I read them, the words evoked an image of excited children dashing out to collect white hail on the grass in a summer storm.

'Oh no.'

'So what sort of food did you eat?'

'Ordinary food. You know, bread, butter, jam . . . Dad grew vegetables. He was a good vegetable gardener. Mother made jam.'

'And fruit trees?'

'Well we had orange trees. She made a Christmas pudding. She made bottles of something. I can see it now, the dark-coloured fruit. People bought the bottles.'

The story of the Christmas puddings was one she had told so often during my childhood that it had become almost iconic. How one year, when they had moved to Umlaas Road, Dad announced that since there was no money there would be no Christmas, and how Mother defied him and set to work on making puddings. Raisins, suet, currants, mixed

128

peel, breadcrumbs, flour, sugar, nutmeg, eggs, brandy ... the recipe in Madge's book is enough for four small ones. She made a long row of puddings and sold each one. The family did have Christmas after all.

'She was an incredible person, really,' my mother said. 'No wonder you see that look on her face. She had a very tough time. To have been brought up in a wealthy family, and then to have to make jam to keep alive ... But if you go on having more and more children, you're asking for a shortage of money. I lost sixpence one day, and that was a terrible thing. We didn't have pocket money. Maybe I was sent to buy something.'

'And what about servants?'

'Yes. A house girl. A young African woman, an *intombi*. She probably lived in a place where African people lived, other side of the railway line. Edendale. I suppose there were odd gardeners too, but I can't remember any of them. Yet there was no sort of race bar. We weren't told not to talk to them or anything.'

As she returned after a lifetime to Blackridge of the 1920s, and the subsequent years dropped away like layers of unwanted clothes, the world she came home to was a place attended by unnamed servants and gardeners who visit the neighbourhood to work, but live somewhere else, just out of sight.

What *was* her name, the young woman who worked for Mrs Smallie? Did she have children of her own? And did she, like other domestic workers in the neighbourhood, have Thursdays as her afternoon off? In Beverley Haddad's work on the spiritual and political activity of the *manyano* – or prayer union – movement, she describes how groups of African women from the area around Blackridge have for decades gathered on Thursdays in one another's homes, to sing and to pray, and to support one another through difficult lives. Set up in the early twentieth century as a local embodiment of the international Mothers' Union, the *manyanos*, as they were soon named, became a powerful site of solidarity and even resistance that the white missionary women who inaugurated the movement could not have anticipated. It was not long before these weekly meetings of the oppressed came to subvert the ethic of 'devout domesticity' which they were intended to inculcate.[41] Did Mrs Smallie's unnamed young employee join the women on the other side of the Ridge on Thursday afternoons to pray? On Sundays, her mistress played the organ in the little white church below the railway line.

'*Angazi*,' my mother said, in isiZulu. 'I don't know.'

The condition of forgetting means you can ask your ageing mother the same question repeatedly and the answers may be different at different times, like the five distinct recipes for Shortbread in Madge's book. But about the lives of black people at Blackridge, it seemed there was nothing left to remember, though I could sometimes glimpse their presence in traces at the edges of things.

'The Johnsons lived above, at the end,' she went on. 'I think they had a shop, what was called a "kaffir" store.'

She gestured the inverted commas in the air.

'Mrs Johnson had big hands. I can see her kneading a loaf of bread, kneading it and kneading it.'

Like Hildagonda Duckitt's 'two nice young fowls, killed the day before', my grandmother's recipes assume a world replete with fresh eggs, live chickens and other domesticated animals, and a housewife competent to turn them into food.

'Oh, we had everything,' my mother said. 'Mother's canaries, and those red hens. Rhode Island Reds. We used to eat them unfortunately – I don't any more – and sell them, and have the eggs. One day the Tatham cousins came to visit. Dad used to call them The Little Rabbits, and Mother used to get furious. There were so many of them, and so close together. There must have been one every six months, if that was possible. Anyway, one Sunday they came with chickenpox. And the chickens got it. Mother lost a lot of those very good white chickens. They were beautiful.'

'Tell us about the bird that pecked the visitor's bottom.'

Sophie and Sky knew the story and wanted to hear it again. They knew too that Granny didn't like the word 'bum'.

'It was a pit latrine, and a bird had a nest in there. Why it wanted to live in there, I don't know. I suppose it was safe. One day there was a yell, and somebody clutching clothes and running for her life.'

'Pecked her bottom?'

'We always hoped for that.'

'And what about the afternoon teas?' I asked.

'Oh! The ladies would have tea at each other's houses, one or two at a time. One was useful carrying cups.'

'What did you eat?'

'Everything homemade. Scones, brown and white scones. Then biscuits and cake. Sandwich cake or fruitcake. If it were some occasion, you would have fruitcake. People would sit and be waited on. We were roped in.'

'And your father?'

'He thought the ladies' teas were *awful*! There was no relaxing. All very tight. You never just dropped in.'

Time and again, whenever I tried to begin a conversation about her mother's cooking, all she could remember were rigid tea parties, joyless foods, and being a girl who had to wash the dishes.

Then one day she simply said, 'Bread and bread and bread and bread . . . She did make lovely bread.'

'You never bought bread?'

'Don't be wicked!'

Suddenly I got the smell of it. How the smell filled the house. The daily bread. Suddenly my grandmother's recipes, which give away nothing of her thoughts except those concerned with the practicalities of home-making, were just the thing to summon from the past a trace of the home she made at Blackridge.

Read this way, the recipe book invoked a sense of the place itself as nothing else could. A big warm range in the kitchen. Slow puddings steaming in a cloth-wrapped basin. Jams simmering in the great brass pan. A boiling kettle. A row of irons. The smell of bread baking, four pounds of flour at a time . . . Yet even as these images combined to conjure the sensory texture of a living scene, I felt the actual kitchen slip away again into nostalgia, lost to the words of it.

'I can see those hot red irons on the stove now,' my mother said. 'The handle had a cloth around it.'

'And what about a fridge?'

'Don't be silly! I remember ice melting all over the place.'

The recipe books bear witness to the fact that, in the years since leaving Sunnyside in Dundee, Madge Smallie née Tatham had learnt to take charge of food, illness, and the tidy maintenance of a household, and that she made things with her own hands that her daughters in their time would buy from the supermarket. The children's teeth were brushed with Family Toothpaste ground in a pestle and mortar and stored in small pots. Floor Polish was a mixture of candle ends and turpentine. She made her own soap.

And she cared for the furniture. This my mother remembered especially. It was solid, heavy, ancestral stuff, she said, and it was always kept spotless and gleaming. My grandmother's polish was made of equal quantities of linseed oil, vinegar, turpentine and naphtha. That scent in the dark wood must have been a key ingredient of the smell of the Blackridge home, the trace of a particular life you take for granted until you leave it behind.

But who could tell what heartbreak was infused in the fragrance, folded into the meticulous order of Madge's house, concealed in the silent gleam of her furniture? When the Boers smashed the pianos and the clocks and paintings of Dundee, the wealthy citizens of the town saw to it that their stolen life was swiftly reconstructed. But after the second devastation when her father died, and she and Alan lost the cattle and the farm, the known world became irretrievable.

For the rest of her life, however diligently she cleaned and shined, she could never match the precarious brilliance of the coal-fuelled years she had lived in the Tatham mansion during the boom time. Though she continued to correct her children's vowels, and made the girls wear gloves in the company of lower-class people on the train, two decades after her family had enjoyed electricity and piped water in Dundee, the little wood-and-iron house at Blackridge was lit with candles and paraffin lamps. It was one of young Betty's jobs to keep the lamps trimmed and clean, and she did not find their light romantic.

8.

'Mother guarded her children like a lioness,' she told me one day. 'Didn't want them to get married. But they escaped past her lion's claws!'

From being the one in the family who climbed trees, made art, wrote poetry, and won prizes at school, Betty left home to attend a teacher's training college in Pietermaritzburg. The family had no money for university. And while she remained fond of them all, soon her liberal values diverged from theirs, and her life took its own course into the world.

She joined the Ramblers, a Natal hiking group, and a tiny photograph from a visit to Cape Town in the 1940s shows her rock-climbing on Table Mountain in shorts and mountain boots, legs spanning the void. After the War, she saved for a year for a berth on a Union Castle liner to

London where she worked at a succession of schools as a supply teacher. On her return to South Africa, Mick Martin, the man she'd gone walking with in the Lake District and who was to become my father, happened to be on the same ship home. The Afrikaner Nationalists had just come into power, and he suggested she apply to join him teaching at the legendary Adams College at Amanzimtoti, where a post was already waiting for him. It was a lively and hopeful place in those early years of apartheid, and they found a kind of home there until 1956, when the devastating implications of the Bantu Education Act came into effect as the government took over the college and the staff resigned in protest. Throughout my childhood, my parents continued to talk about the Adams days, but by that time my mother was teaching at Epworth Junior School in Pietermaritzburg, an educational environment inspired by sixties experimental pedagogy, where she worked hard to nurture children's imaginations. By then, she no longer climbed mountains, but she still loved hiking in the wild, she loved living creatures, she loved to make things with her hands, and she remained distinctly independent-minded. In retirement, they moved to Cape Town, and after my father's death she gathered around her a group of devoted friends who were mostly quite a bit younger than she was. We began getting together for her birthday each year, each time wondering if it would be the last. One evening, as someone stood up to make a speech, she interrupted with mock firmness, 'Now I don't want to hear another person calling me a free spirit.'

Yet in her final years, dementia had made her an exile. The world contracted to the space of a single room, a lifetime of people and activity was erased from her mind, and her friends found it increasingly difficult to relate to her. While for most of her life she might well choose solitude as a lively creative space, she now felt lonely, as she'd never done before, trapped in a fog of forgetting. Out of this condition, the family she had left behind returned as ghosts. Mother. Dad. Cyril. Blackridge.

One afternoon we were looking at old photographs of her brothers and sisters when she said, 'I've got a funny feeling of being plucked off a branch like a fruit. So now I'm my own person.'

'Why do you think that is?'

'We were all a mishmash . . . and now we're separated out. A little bit lonely. Gosh, Julie, it's terribly lonely here. That's what made me hesitate to come and live here. You know, my memory's so awful. Just yesterday I thought, "I must ring up Mother." Still on my mind.'

I had explained earlier that her mother died fifty years before. Usually, it seemed more helpful to tell her. Cut through the anxiety. She would be surprised, blame herself for forgetting, and then relax for a while, relieved.

In all our conversations, the impression she gave of my grandmother was of someone whose continual busyness would have left little time for reading. But apart from the recipe collections, the only other book that she passed from Madge's hands into mine was a novel, its thick old pages bound in red, the title embossed in gold: *A Woman of Small Account* by Mary Martens.

The novel was published in 1911, and my grandmother's inscription, dated 1913, records that it was a gift from her husband. A little research revealed that, when they were young, the author and my grandparents must have been part of the same social set, possibly girlhood friends. Mary had also lived in Dundee, and her brother had been mayor of the town a few years after WH Tatham. Once the South African War was over, she'd married a Boer farmer.

After so many recipes, the novel is quite startling. Like the other farmers' wives, Mary Martens would have known well enough how to bake and to make soap. But the book she wrote is a fierce critique of the domestication of women and speaks out strongly for women's power. In the same year that the Pankhursts were taking to the streets in England, and a small group of suffragists met in Durban to launch the Women's Enfranchisement Association of the Union, her novel made its own emphatic assertion.[42] It was subtitled *A South African Social Picture*, and was nothing at all like a recipe book. Instead of the eternal repetitions of bread-making, mending, polishing furniture, and washing the dishes, the story she tells is precisely situated in time and place, and full of individual women who are anything but compliant.

Early on, she calls Hester, her main character, a suffragist in embryo.

135

Like many a young maiden in a *plaasroman*, she lives on a farm in the colony and falls in love with a cosmopolitan man who visits from overseas. But, like Madge's own story, this particular narrative does not end with a wedding. After the marriage, Hester's life contracts depressingly into the narrow domain of a house in Pietermaritzburg, where the bright young woman who used to write articles for a journal called *Woman's Sphere* becomes a listless wife whose husband goes out to work.

When at last she begins to write again, things change. This time it is a novel about the sexual abuse of black women by white men in South Africa. Her husband considers it a shameful book, but Hester refuses to be suppressed. Even before her marriage, she had felt trapped by her social role as a woman:

> 'I feel like a caged bird,' mused she in bitter tone. 'I want to be up and doing something to lend my small weight to the struggle. My life is cramped and narrow. I beat my limbs against bars that seem to hold and pinion me. And I dare not speak aloud, or my relations would think me mad as well as wicked.'[43]

So when her husband forbids her to continue writing, she fearlessly challenges the power relations between them: 'When you brought me here,' she says, 'it was as your wife and equal I came, not as your subordinate, and the bondswoman to your wishes.'[44] Against his wishes – and at the cost of her marriage – Hester goes on to publish the novel and to achieve fame for its role in promoting 'the big social reform movement'.[45]

What could this subversive and sentimental narrative have meant for my grandmother? Like Hester, she was a strong and determined woman. But while Hester wrote consciousness-raising fiction, Madge recorded recipes. Hester walked out on her husband and travelled the world, while Madge made food and cleaned the house and raised a large family. Hester challenged social hierarchies, while Madge hankered for the lost privileges of her girlhood. And while Hester was passionate and outspoken, Madge would not bring herself to express her feelings, and punished her daughters when they did.

Yet the novel was one of the few possessions my grandmother carried with her for the rest of her life from one home to the next as the family grew and dispersed, the animals were born and died, and her living space diminished until at last she lived alone in a small rented house in Pieter-maritzburg. It also seemed to be the single work of fiction that my mother had saved from her eldest sister Letty's possessions after her death. Later, as her own life contracted from a flat to a retirement complex to the nursing home room where she now lay, *A Woman of Small Account* was one of the objects that remained.

Letty and Betty were to live into their nineties, but their mother died at seventy-three. She had met her husband when she was a schoolgirl and, what with six children (and a seventh who died unmentioned by the family, but was noted in a church record as '*infant of Mrs Smallie*'), there was no question of tertiary education or a career, or writing a novel, or even a diary.

Was Madge Smallie a caged bird? At Blackridge, she bred canaries.

My mother told the story for the first time after we returned from looking for the house and I mentioned the eucalyptus plantation on the Ridge.

'Oh my father planted gum trees,' she said. 'They grew quickly and easily. Well, Mother used to breed canaries on the front verandah, and Dad made her a big aviary. I didn't like them because I had to look after them. One day I let them out by mistake. And they *flew* up to the top of the gum trees.'

'What did she do?'

'I can't remember what happened, but I remember the awfulness of it. And that last bird. All that was left . . . The little blue eggs were very nice. There was a shelter at the top of the aviary, and that was where they had their babies.'

'You've always disliked birds in cages.'

'I didn't like the whole thing. And also, I didn't like having to look after them. Somebody let them out. It wasn't me, I was very careful. Mother thought it was me, I suppose. But it . . . wasn't me. Towards evening, some of them came back. Perhaps all of them.'

After this conversation, the canaries became a memory she returned to often.

'It was a duty,' she said on another visit. 'Mother's canaries. And I hated it, really. I like to think that I felt birds shouldn't be kept in cages. I still don't like the idea of birds being kept in cages.'

She was lying as she always lay, propped against pillows, the cot sides of the hospital bed up, and her legs tied to the blue cushion to keep them from crossing. Confined to her bed, she garnered what freedom she could from the syringa tree and its creatures, and from writing poems in a messy notebook. In all weathers, she insisted on keeping the glass doors to the verandah open.

'Now you've got the pigeons,' I said.

'Oh Julie,' she said, beaming. 'The pigeons are amazing! They are nice, very nice. And they come and go as they want to. And I like that. Those little canaries of Mother's were very sweet, but I didn't like them. When I come to think about it, she should have looked after them. She was a strange person. I suppose she was of her time. You know, this pigeon is cleaning every single feather he's got. I'm enjoying being in this room. I'm going to stay here.'

9.

I called the only Tegg in Pietermaritzburg, and managed to track down someone who knew him.

'Yes, that's Graham Tegg,' the woman's voice said. 'He's difficult to get hold of. You could try and leave a message.' Then, about the wood-and-iron house, 'Yes he lives in that old house in Thorpe Lane. I don't think he's done much with the place.'

With Mr Tegg's number in hand, so close now to some kind of resolution, I began to feel apprehensive. Why 'difficult'? Did I imagine that pause, something unsaid? And why the other comment about the house?

The phone rang for a while, until it was answered by the recording of a man's voice, slow and tetchy: 'I don't know what you're talking about. I've no idea.'

I left a message, not very hopefully. He sounded like someone short on tolerance, possibly even hostile, a man living on his own in an old house, the hundred-year-old corrugated iron rusting away, and the garden grown tall about him, a shelter from strangers.

'Don't expect to get a response,' Michael said.

That evening, the phone rang: 'Hello, Graham speaking.'

It took me a moment. Graham. Tegg. Wow.

'Oh yes, hello! I'm so glad to hear from you. Let me call you back.'

I told him all of it from the beginning and he listened. Listened so quietly, in fact, that it made me go on and on, filling the silence, hoping that my assumption of trust would evoke an answering trust in him.

When at last I was done, I gave him a cue to respond, 'What do you think of that?'

'Yes,' he said, thoughtfully. 'Well there's our place (I think it was owned by the Railways at some point). And there's also another very old house at the same level, closer to Sweetwaters Road.'

'Really? Just below the railway line?'

'Yes. And if she says it was quite a walk to the station and the church, then maybe it was more likely to have been that one.'

'And it's the same sort of age as your house? Wood and iron?'

'Yes.'

'And you wouldn't be able to see it from the road?'

'No. The plot was subdivided, like this one. There's a very narrow driveway up towards the house. People we knew used to stay there.'

That Maritzburg accent. He sounded like my uncles and aunts. I knew his voice, but what he was saying was remarkable. Having zoomed in on Google Maps to what was probably his house, a little square structure with a verandah all around, not far from where the station used to be, I'd more or less given up the idea of its being The One. But if there were another house, nearby . . .

'That's amazing. And are there big trees around it? My mother always talks about the trees. Her father planted gum trees.'

'Yes, lots of big trees. And gum trees over that way, yes.'

'I remember seeing them from the railway line.'

'They pulled up the railway line during our time, you know.'

'Really, that recently? When was that?'

'Oh I don't know, couldn't say. There also used to be, years ago, a roadway on the side of us. They would go up on their horses, army guys, to report to some general or something. So it goes back donkey's years.'

'Up to the Ridge? When my mother was a little girl, it was still wild up on the hill, lots of grasses. They used to walk up there.'

'Some people call it progress,' he said, 'but I don't.'

I mentioned our friend Wally Menne's insistence on making the distinction between a forest and a plantation.

'Yes, that's it. We have a lovely view from here, both forest and plantation. But the plantations spoil it.'

He continued, telling me about his property, 'It must have been a *beautiful* place in its day. They subdivided it, you know, several properties.'

'Someone wanted to make money.'

'Yes. But I've found paths made of old bricks. Quite deep down, buried under layers of soil. One of them is a pathway right across into my neighbour's garden. It used to be one property, you see, and the path went to the tennis court. The new house was built over it.'

'They must have been wealthy. My mother's never mentioned a tennis court.'

'Yes. But maybe the other house.'

'Maybe. And what about a stream? Is there a stream? She always talks about a stream.'

'A couple, yes. One near us, and another, I think, towards that other house. Big trees too. There are some very big trees here. I did have to cut some down. Very reluctantly. I did cut some.'

It felt like a confession.

'It's still lovely around there, though,' I said. 'It must be a good place to live.'

'Yes, it is.'

Buried pathways, big trees, a stream ... We talked, as they say, the same language. His kindness admonished my fears.

I thanked him, said how glad I was to meet him, and that I'd written him a letter earlier in the day, which was lying, stamped and addressed, on the table before me. Would he still like to see it?

'Oh send it anyway. You took all the trouble to write it, so don't waste it.'

'And the other house? Do you have any idea of the street number?'

'No ... but I could find out.'

'Thank you again.'

'Okay then my dear,' he ended off, 'good luck with it all.'

I called my mother straight away.

'Do you remember a tennis court at Blackridge?'

'Tennis court. Well, the people next door ... Oh I can't remember. Maybe there was a tennis court somewhere.'

I told her about the conversation with Graham Tegg, and the possibility of another house.

She said, 'It makes me feel a bit homesick.'

'I know. But you're glad I'm doing this?'

'Oh yes, very.'

'And when you say "homesick", what does that mean for you?'

'Homesick? It's losing something that has been yours. Losing your surroundings that you've lived with and taken for granted. And gradually, gradually getting used to the new conditions.'

She paused, and then continued, 'Remembering very well, and wishing to go back, actually. The place where you grew up. That's it. You probably (I don't know about this, but…), you probably remember things that were good and forget things that were difficult.'

'It's fascinating how important a particular place can be for us.'

'I know. They are.'

'Maybe we won't find the actual house, but perhaps that doesn't really matter. It's the process that's interesting, what turns up on the way.'

'I would be very surprised, really, if it were still there. I mean, it *was* there! The back verandah had a trelliswork (I think I'm right) up the back. It's a fascinating thing you're doing.'

A few nights later the phone rang. Graham Tegg. I called him back.

'Well I've got some bad news for you, and some good news. Okay, first the bad news. Looking at the photo, our house doesn't suit this one at all. Ours is flat on the ground, but your mom's one is elevated.'

'Right, and she talks about crawling under the house.'

The dark place under the house had become a core location in my mother's memory, and a deciding element for me in tracking the place down.

'But you know what you also need to look at is the horizon of the hill behind. I got my oldest camera, it's an instamatic,' he laughed, 'and I looked in the viewfinder. From our place, looking up at the hill, it's really quite high behind the house, much higher than in the photo of your mom's house. If you look you can see that the chap who took the picture must have been standing on a drum or a step-ladder or something. He's above the steps.'

'Okay, yes I can see that.'

I'd found the scanned photograph on my computer while he was talking.

'But even so, the roof is higher than the horizon, and you just wouldn't get that angle around here. The house must have been quite a bit further down the line. That hill being as low as it is, it has to be a fair way down. If you look to the left of the house, near that fir tree or whatever, you can see it's quite flattish ground, quite a big bit of flattish level ground around the house.'

I could see what he meant. He went on to point out that the picture was taken from an angle about forty degrees or so to the side of the house.

'And you see that blind pulled down in the front? They've got the same sort of problem as we have.'

'Morning sun?'

'Yes. So that gives you the orientation.'

I asked him about the picture of the stand of wild-looking bush below the line near the site of the station that my mother loved especially. Could it be a remnant of indigenous forest?

'Well,' he thought about it, 'there are some trees that have been introduced too. I think it belongs to the Railways. When I first came here, I used to go there. Some people used to set snares for the monkeys, so I would go in and dismantle the snares. I remember there were two old-fashioned corrugated iron water tanks there, but never any sign of old buildings. I was interested because I like that sort of thing.'

'Anyway, when I'm stronger, when I've got all my wits about me, I'll take a look down that way, further down.'

'Oh. Have you not been well?'

'I've suddenly got old. I'm sixty-one and I ended up getting a stroke. Didn't expect it, but that's what happened.'

'I'm so sorry. Have you been disabled at all?'

'On the one side a bit, but it's coming right. And the speech a bit. But I'm getting better, very well looked after.'

'Well you sound good. And such incredible attention to detail. Looking at the photo . . . you're such a good reader.'

'Oh . . .' he laughed. 'Just a curious mind. But the biggest clue we've got is that horizon. See if you can find another photo that can help us with the background, with the hill. It might just help us along.'

Us. We. I was moved. Yet again, someone I'd never met before had generously responded to my quest, taken it on.

After speaking to him, I posted a heap of letters to 'The Resident', sending them to all the neighbouring addresses, with the picture of the house. I explained that it might in fact be quite a bit further down the line than Thorpe Lane, but hidden from view among big trees.

Within a couple of days, a call came in from someone called Willie Schoeman. Like Graham he'd applied his full attention to the photograph.

'I've been looking at that ridge,' he said. 'I think, from where I am now, we're just a bit out, but there's the same line of the hill in the background. It follows the line completely. So I'll investigate for you, see if we can make some sense of this for you. I'll ask my son. If there's anything, he'll know it. He knows the area really well.'

'Thank you, I'm so touched. It's a strange sort of quest, but do you understand?'

'Oh yes absolutely. One hundred per cent.'

10.

Whenever my mother spoke about forgetting things because they were difficult, it made me wonder what had happened to her memory of my father. My brilliant, playful, generous father. She had shared more than forty years of life with him, but now not even an echo of his name remained. Michael Martin. Mick.

He finished school at sixteen, and at seventeen, after tricking his way into the army by memorising the eye test, he was shipped off to North Africa.

The poems he sent home to his mother found their way into anthologies of twentieth-century war poetry, but when I finally took the books off the shelf to read them, my interest was personal. Perhaps the poems held some portent of the loss that was to come. His comrades in the campaign may have garnered some relief through the usual distractions and denials, but my father's poems suggest that Private Martin, Signaller, was staring open-eyed into hell. In mid-1942, as the Eighth Army made enthusiastic preparations for a heroic destruction of the enemy, his words witness unambiguously to the bleak horror of the desert war, and his sensitive young mind is precisely conscious of the damage that it is receiving:

VOICE OF THE LIBYAN DESERT
June 1942

I am the death to your dreams of romance,
I am the blight and the running sore;
I am the sand that blinds your eyes,
I am the setting for total war.

145

I grow no corn and I store no hay,
Take heed you soldiers who come my way.

My sun is a molten blistering ball,
Striking men down, and striking men dead;
My winter's a toothless, frosty hag,
Slithering into your dusty bed.

I stalk by night and I storm by day,
Take heed you soldiers who come my way.

My friends the flies, in their billions ten,
My furnace-child, the Khamseen brings;
They come to poison the food of men,
Gloating death, on myriad wings.

I forge my weapons in decay;
Take heed you soldiers who come my way.

I know no bonds and I keep no laws,
I am not tamed, and I am not yours;
I'll dim your eyes, and I'll close your pores,
And I'll grind you in my terrible jaws.

My words are grim: Enough, I say,
Take heed you soldiers who come my way.[46]

It was, of course, a warning that few could hear and none could heed.

On the eve of the Battle of El Alamein, a few months after he wrote these words, the men were informed by their commanders that the forthcoming conflict would change the course not only of the war, but of history. The issue at stake was beyond all calculation, the generals told them, and all must do their utmost, no matter what the cost.[47]

For my father, just nineteen years old, the cost was uncountable. After what was indeed a decisive victory for the Allies, he was hospitalised in Alexandria. Nervous breakdown, they said. These days the *DSM-5* would call it PTSD, but at that time it was a form of injury whose sufferers did not make it into the list of casualties that my grandfather AC Martin recorded in his two-volume official history of the Durban Light Infantry. It must have been an ignominious end to the war for the colonel's gifted son.

The experience was not something my father spoke about, but it seems to me in retrospect that the shock of it remained with him for the rest of his life, and affected us all.

If my mother appeared to have forgotten him completely, the man I remember would read to me at night, and play the piano while I sang, speak radiant lines of Keats or TS Eliot from memory, walk about the house conducting symphonies in the early mornings, and stand below the syringa tree with his arms wide open to catch me when I jumped. His incandescent mind was playful and inventive and kind. He had a fine sense of the ridiculous. He loved cats. Nothing was happier than his irresistible laugh.

And then there was depression. That terrible shadowing of unpredictable darkness into which, after his time in the Western Desert, he periodically withdrew. Always it came back. After weeks or months of this affliction, when he finally left his bed in the darkened room and the world became luminous again, he never failed to think, hope, pray that he had somehow routed the depression for good. That he'd found the secret. And then one day his face would change, his voice lose its verve, his body slump.

I used to imagine it must be that he'd become imprisoned in a kind of vast sadness. But what did I know, except that once again I'd lost him.

That my mother loved him, I never doubted. It was a comfort, too, that where he was labile, she seemed steadfast, enduring the impact of his illnesses with real fortitude. But after the car knocked him down in the street at the age of sixty-eight, and he lay for ten days in a coma in the ICU while I sang him the songs of our ancestors – I thought he would die but she was determined, my mother, that her husband should live – after all that, when he did in fact come back to life, at first ecstatic and newborn as Blake's 'Infant Joy', then utterly desperate saying die die die, and then simply frail and much much older, an ancient man delivered utterly into her hands, his brain injured, his body weak, his heart open and loving, more tender than ever before, and after he then lived two more years and finally died of pneumonia . . . after all that infinite care and patience and exhaustion, in her old age the memory of her husband, my father, simply slipped out of sight.

Who knows why.

11.

Autumn came, season of mists, and I realised I was sick. After a day of it, I took to my bed, clogged up with snot and washed through with a sadness of my own that could no longer be contained.

As I lay alone, the Blackridge project tracked back and forth through the mind, racked with impossible questions. Why is she still in the nursing home? What if we move her somewhere else? Why can't we have her at home? Why am I still looking for a vanished house? Are we now trapped together in the cage of her delusion, the desiccations of old age? What can I do with this sadness?

Lying in the darkened bedroom, the curtains drawn to keep out the light, I longed for a narrative of completeness, some orderly tale to take care of the anguish. How deft her fingers used to be, sewing bright pictures of trees and birds, girls and boys, a little house. As a child, I'd watch her hands working and know I'd never be able to sew like that. But now her basket of silk threads was a tangled mess in the nursing home cupboard, and my feverish dreams kept returning to the dark room at the centre of the house. And the death of dogs.

It was at just this time that an email came in about two great black dogs who seemed to be quite real as well as mythic. Heiko Bron, who ran a neighbourhood newsletter for Blackridge, had included my request about a second wood-and-iron house in his circular, adding his own suggestion. It read: 'There is another hidden house which has a long driveway, and that is at the lower end of Highfield Road adjacent to the abandoned railway line as well. As I have never seen that house, I cannot tell whether it is made from corrugated iron. It is where the black Belgian Alsatians reside.'

In my sick state, those pitch-black dogs in their forest of high trees became a sort of visitation from the deep. Black dogs were living at the wood-and-iron house again. Alsatians. There was something especially uncanny about that word 'reside'. Not sure how much of it I was imagining, I passed on Heiko's description without comment to Colin Gardner. He wrote back at once that they sounded like something out of a Grimm's fairy tale.

Meanwhile, I'd not been able to visit my mother, and her phone calls became increasingly distressed.

'I feel as though there's a black cloud,' she said one day. 'As though I've come to a big wall. I feel as though there's a crisis of some sort and I don't know what it is . . . Why do I feel I should be somewhere else?'

I tried explaining that the feelings of displacement, disorientation, or simply wanting to be at home – even if you're already there – are quite common in dementia.

'But why am I so stupid?'

'You're really not at all stupid.'

'Can I be here always? Can I *die* here?'

'Yes. Does that feel like a relief?'

'Yes, strangely. Though I don't want to die now.'

Next day, a panicked, angry, agitated phone call told me the opposite.

'I want to leave this terrible place! I'm bored and lonely. I want to go home.'

'Where's that?'

'Oh you know . . . Where I used to live before.'

We went through the usual range of topics: you've been at the nursing home for several years, it's where you live now, and so on.

'But I'm not going to live *here* for the rest of my life!' she said, quite desperately. 'I'm not going to die here! I've been *counting the days* to today, because I thought this was when I was coming home.'

I explained that she needed care ('I don't!'), that she was unable to walk ('I just need a stick!') and so on. I also tried to explain that I myself was now sick in bed, so I couldn't come to see her. But she simply swept on in an angry storm of words that made her unable to hear what I was saying.

150

'Okay,' I finally said. 'I'll make some calls.'

I phoned her doctor. What to do?

We both knew that the place where she was staying was problematic. Apart from the fact that the nurses were underpaid and demoralised, and that Mrs D disapproved of feeding pigeons, there had been various incidents that caused us some disquiet. Yet even so, the doctor, whose care and experience I trusted, felt sure there was no real alternative.

'I think you'll see a marked degeneration if you move her now,' she said.

'Really? Even though she's so unhappy where she is?'

'Yes really.'

Still, I felt quite desperate, probably more so than usual, with the virus bringing a sweaty vulnerability into the mix. So I called a different nursing home I'd heard good things about, and spoke to a friendly sounding matron. Yes certainly, she told me, they would consider my mother for Frail Care and put her in a room with three other people.

I simply couldn't imagine it. For all her present loneliness, she had become fiercely resistant to making new friends. She wanted privacy. She wanted her own space. And she wanted her family. The people she knew.

When I called her back, she began to berate me again. It was all the same anguish and distress, on and on in the same vein. I simply started crying. Couldn't help it.

Her reaction was instantaneous. At once she became sensible and reassuring. Suddenly, the mother I remembered, the containing presence, was there again.

'You see,' she said, in a completely different voice, 'one fights against this, and that makes one very unpleasant. It isn't fun to be ninety-two. But you've just got to deal with it. I apologise now for the fact that I am such a . . . a forgetter.'

And then, again, 'It *will* come right. I'll do all the dealing, and I'll try and hold you up.'

This was exactly what the small child in me wanted to hear. That somewhere, somehow, she still had the capacity to take care of me. I knew, of course, that tomorrow would be a different story, that there was really no solid ground at all. But just for a moment it felt like home, like the lullaby she used to sing.

'Now you remember about that skirt?' she went on. 'But don't stop at a skirt. I want you to have a beautiful top, too. Just buy it if you don't want to make it.'

It was my mother, seeing to it that I was clothed, and beautifully so. And this from someone whose own mother didn't think she should have pretty things.

'If I don't do anything else,' she said, 'I want you to be all right. None of this would be anything without you.'

By the end of the conversation, she seemed completely happy.

'I feel like crowing,' she said, 'I feel so good.'

12.

It was Friday and the nurse set a bleak plate of lunch down on the yellow-wood tray my grandfather Alan had made a century before.

'I'm not going to eat that!' my mother said emphatically.

At Blackridge when she didn't like the cooked meal she was supposed to finish, she would bury it in the ground. Everyone else was too busy to notice. It was one advantage of being low in the family hierarchy, or what they called a nuisance. Betty was small and she learnt how to slip out of view. Out of the house and into the garden.

Now her escape was simply to refuse to eat.

'What do you think they've *done* to that fish?' she said, looking at the plate. 'I can see it swimming through the water.'

'Why not eat some of the vegetables?'

'This food . . . it's one of the problems of this place.'

'What's wrong with it?'

'No affection.'

It was the same word she had used about her mother. Not much affection.

Food and love. Love and food.

Another time, as I put a bunch of red globe grapes into her hands as we arrived at the bedside, she lit up and said, 'Oh we used to pick grapes at Blackridge! We used to pick long lines of grapes, at the other end of the ground. Catawbas, the black ones.'

'What about mangoes?'

'Gorgeous! Mangoes.' She was still smiling. 'And hot mealies with butter, absolutely glorious. The white ones. Nothing like it.'

'And other food?'

'No.' Her smiled dropped. 'Mother didn't like cooking.'

Mother and food and love. This repetition. Somehow, she found her way out.

For all the carefully recorded recipes that she came to inherit, the home food she really loved was something she discovered herself as a small girl, outside the family house. The taste of it was to remain with her as a defining joy for the rest of her life: fruits picked from the garden.

Now, after its passage through more than a hundred years of kitchens, the copy of Hilda's "Where Is It?" that I received from her – who inherited it from her sister Letty, who had it from Mother – is broken at the spine, the pages loose from their stitching, mottled with age and marked like all good recipe books with patches of fat and stuck flour, dark liquid spills, and the burn from an ember. When the original beige cloth cover became so stained that the title was almost illegible, someone sewed a loose linen one. Now it too was frayed and old, a faded design of anemones, pinks and narcissus. English favourites.

Hildagonda Duckitt would have appreciated the fabric. She loved food, but she also loved flowers, and in both she seems to have enjoyed a Victorian taste for collecting and dissemination. In 1891, the same year that her popular recipe book was first published and shipped across the Empire, she gathered a handful of Nemesia strumosa seeds from the Darling area where she lived, and posted them to a nursery in England. The flowers were extraordinary, bright as butterflies, reds, oranges, yellows, and pinks, each colour distinctive from the different farms. A century later, the same wild nemesias are now under threat in their native district from industrial agriculture, alien encroachment, and other symptoms of progress. But the small packet of seeds Hilda gathered on the farm was to germinate multitudes of descendants, and became one of global horticulture's most popular annuals, available at nurseries everywhere, long after her book was forgotten.

My grandmother's own handwritten recipe collection is still in use. When my mother inherited the transmission and had the book rebound, she indexed the contents and began writing her own recipes for foods that increasingly diverged from the sort of cuisine with which she had grown up. Like Madge's, the entries are not concerned with public or

154

even family events, though reading them now in the aged book – its pages specked and marked like the arms of an old woman who has spent her youth in the sun – my heart is full of childhood. At 330 entries, the book is nearly full, but whatever tales the numbered sequence might be asked to tell, its contents are not so much stories as instructions for repeatable events, recurrent as the memory of home: a Christmas cake each year, plain scones for tea, chocolate cake for a birthday, muffins for the children's lunch at school. Like the seeds of a wild nemesia sent across the world, the family recipes loop and return. Their teaching is dense, explicit, tangible as bread.

Yet if Madge's book has more to do with the rituals of care and home-making in the colonies than with history, even family history, the single event to which it does bear witness was decisive. In the new Index, my mother wrote the only contemporary record I have found of my grandmother's death. Between Recipe 266 for Shortbread (Edith's), and Recipe 267 for Biscuits (Plain), the pivotal moment is recorded in three words neatly inscribed in black ink and underlined twice: 'After August 1956'. To which she later added, in blue ballpoint, 'when Mother died'.

Half a century later in the nursing home, the seemingly indelible imprint of Madge Smallie's life had almost obliterated the fact of her death. When almost everything else was lost, the fact of Mother remained and continued to repeat, perennial as women's work, or the need to be fed. Mother and mother and mother and bread and bread and bread.

'How's Mother?' she would continue to ask, nearly every day. 'I wonder if Mother would like that plant . . . If Mother doesn't want it, you can have it.'

When I hesitated, she would say, 'Has Mother died? *Why didn't you tell me?*'

'Yes,' I would explain again, 'She died. More than fifty years ago.'

She would be surprised, sad, sometimes relieved. For the rest of the visit she might remember it.

'You see,' she said one day, 'the floor was linoleum, polished. Not a thing out of place. She demanded perfect work. Looking back, there's a lot that I would have liked different. And this curious marriage . . .

I heard Dad say to Doodie once, "You must stand up for yourself. Don't let Mother rule you all the time." It's all very well. She was a very demanding woman. She preferred the boys of course. The girls were just a nuisance.'

Then she added, her mother's fifth and most unruly child, 'You can be as dramatic as you like when you're writing about this. My memory is full of blotches, like ink left about and knocked over.'

13.

'I just want to say thank you *very* much,' she said, beaming. 'You've brought me full circle to Blackridge.'

I realised that, for the moment, she believed she was actually there. Then she read the uncertainty on my face, and hesitated.

'Or Blackridge area . . .'

I didn't know what to say.

'Well what do *you* call Blackridge? This is where we used to live.'

Next day, she was agitated, worrying about trains.

'I don't know how it works, but I can't *think*. I can't even visualise Maritzburg. I can't fix my brain properly at all.'

'You know, some people get this at seventy or eighty, or even much younger. You're ninety-two and doing pretty well.'

'Do you want me to stay where I am?'

'Yes.'

'It's quite frightening, really . . . I must just know that this is where I belong?'

'Yes.'

'Theoretically, I knew that Mother had died, but I don't remember it.'

'It doesn't matter.'

'I must just know that I haven't got to catch a train or anything?'

This time, she was anxious rather than actually hallucinating that she was on a train.

'How do you mean?'

'Well, if you don't catch a train, then it puts other people out.'

As she spoke, she became more distressed, breath coming fast, and it was an effort not to be infected by her state.

'Now tell me what I must do!'

About five times then, she asked this, my mother who had always re-
sisted anyone telling her what to do.

'You must just be,' I said, using her own term, and making the effort
to relax my own breath. 'Watch the pigeons. Look at that long branch
of the syringa tree. This is where you live.'

'I must get it clear in my mind that I do live here,' she responded,
'and I will live here. I planned that Julie should get herself material for a
skirt and make it.'

'That's me, and yes I will do it. I've been sick, but I'm better now and
I'll do it.'

'Yes, that's one good thing.'

Yet again, I was reminded that dementia has no linear teleology. Its
patterns are recursive: loops and tangles, recipes that repeat and repeat,
stories myelinated by repetition, railway lines that keep on tracking
through a life and tie your stomach in a knot, old paths in the mind, full
circle.

I wrote a list of our habitual topics of conversation and it made my
mother laugh. Then I asked her about the stream.

'What was it like?'

'Oh . . .' she smiled. 'It ran across somewhere fairly high up, on the
station side of the plot, and made its way across. It was a real storybook
stream, with willow trees here and there right up close to the river. We
could play there – it was considered very safe. Safety was a bit of a thing
out there . . . People watched carefully those who walked alone. Whether
anything actually happened, I don't know. You wouldn't go walking
alone to the station for instance if you were a little person.'

'What would you play in the stream?'

'Paddle. It was a clean little stream, really a small stream, not deep. It
ran between two decent bits of grass and wild flowers. It sounds like a
carpet, now, the back garden. Actual mealie fields, you can imagine. They
were wonderful, enough for us to pick and eat. There's nothing on earth
like a mealie grown in your own back yard.'

'And the stream itself?'

'It wasn't a river, really. We called it a river, but it was quite a decent stream. The stream ran on, down and round, past a dam and into the sea.'

'The sea?' I was surprised. 'The sea was quite far away.'

'Yes, but the beach wasn't so very, very far.'

Who cares about accuracy when you are speaking about love?

'And wild flowers, of course,' she went on.

'Can you remember particular flowers?'

'I've never seen it anywhere else – a fluffy head of blue.'

'Cope's Folly. We saw them when we were there.'

'Oh lovely, actually in flower?'

'Yes.'

'And there were Mother's canaries on the verandah of course. It was grim, the thought that those little things should be flying about. But in those days, people didn't think from the bird's point of view.'

She paused and smiled. 'Gosh I love this project because it makes it alive again. I had a nasty nightmare, but I can't remember it now. So that's just as well . . . And how are you? Is everyone all right?'

I told her that Sky and Michael were building a treehouse.

'Oh, that was a thing we used to talk about, Cyril and I. We never made one, but we always thought how wonderful it would be. You know, if it hadn't been for Cyril, I don't think I would have enjoyed anything really.'

During the strange vague days of her condition, when most of the recent past found no hold in the memory, a few particular things from the immediate present held on tight.

'Have you done anything about that skirt?' she asked me again, on another visit.

'I will, I want to . . .'

'I forget everything except that skirt. Now tell me, has Mother died?'

'Yes.'

'And Dad?'

'Yes.'

'And Letty?'

'Yes, all of them.'

'There's this awful feeling of not being yourself at all. Can't *think*.'

'Your kindness is still there. And your wisdom.'

'Well my wisdom is hanging on a thread. There are some lovely flowers in my room. And that gorgeous peacock feather. It's absolutely beautiful. Thank goodness for growing things, for plants and flowers, and for birds. For animals, we are especially lucky.'

Beauty nearly always brought her back, the sparkling joy of living things.

The next time she asked me, I simply said, 'They've all died.'

She seemed grateful as well as sad.

Then she went on, 'Why haven't I? I should have. I should have had the sense. I wouldn't mind dying, but it seems as far away as that mountain . . . If I want to come home, what can I do? I won't be any trouble.'

Whenever she spoke in this way, I had the agonising sense that she was repeating a childhood experience of having been excluded from the family, or feeling she was a nuisance to her mother and the older siblings. But this time she didn't wait for an answer.

'I want you to do me a favour,' she said. 'Get a little notebook, and write "d" next to the ones who've died. And for God's sake *you* stay alive. And when I go, don't fret.'

Later that evening, when I called to say goodnight, she said, 'Julie, do come and visit me some time?'

'Yes, I will. And I do visit you, quite often. It's just that you forget.'

'What did I do to deserve this *horror* of a memory?'

'It's a brain thing, a brain disease. Not your fault at all. It's quite common at your age.'

'Got a bit dried out or something?' she laughed.

Perhaps suffering and love are inextricable. Perhaps all we can ever change is our response. Release and breathe out. Each time.

'You know,' she continued, 'this peacock feather you brought me – I didn't remember the name till you told me – it's *incredibly* beautiful. And *please* get your skirt made?'

14.

The long days rolled on, recursive and uncalendared. And then two things happened that quite simply and decisively released me from the quest. First, it was the land invasion. And then I sang the lullaby again.

It had turned out that the house hidden in the forest where the black dogs reside was of recent construction, and the heap of kind messages I received from the Blackridge neighbours made it clear that there was no other house built of wood and iron. But it was the email from Francois that really signalled the conclusion to my search.

In March 2010, he mentioned in passing, 'There has been a land invasion last week in the area.'

I could find no report of it in the local newspaper, or anywhere online, and wrote to him immediately for more. He replied that no, the action had not been documented, but that it began in the second week of March and after ten days the Msunduzi Municipality obtained a High Court interdict to move people off the land.

When I pressed further, he wrote back: 'Yes it was there in Blackridge right next to the surveyed and registered properties. On a piece of public land below the forested area and next to the old railway line that we walked on. Just more to the southeast. Winter sky (hazy) is setting in and the grass is starting to yellow, the first fires are being burned to make fire breaks.'

I called the municipality but it was difficult to get more details, and Francois remained my best source of information. I wrote to him that on Google Maps I could see quite a big open space below Albany Road, near where Uplands Road comes to an end. It looked as though people living not far away in the Caluza Road area might easily move over there.

He replied that, yes, the site of the land invasion was at the end of Uplands Road and below Albany Road, next to the old line: Erf 518 PMB, surveyed after the arrival of the railway. In the late 1880s the land was granted to the Botanical Society and held with a trust. At one or other stage, he said, the municipality got it back and planted trees on the top half up against the slope. They had to get special permission to close the public place. But the bottom half had remained open and cattle grazed there from time to time. He concluded with the words, 'The claimants believe that their Chief has a right because his cattle grazed there in the past.'

Cattle grazing. We had seen them. They must have been moving through for generations.

I contacted John Wright for a better sense of who lived in the region before the colonial occupation. He wrote back that before 1820 the Nqondo people lived in the Edendale valley on the other side of the Ridge. Then, in the early 1820s, various groups from further north in the Midlands came pushing south, no doubt destabilising the Southern Midlands and Southern Natal. In the 1830s, the Mpumuza, the Zondi, and the Nxamalala moved in from the middle Thukela region under pressure from Dingane and settled near Swartkop, the mountain overlooking the valley a few kilometres to the northwest of Blackridge hill. They were mixed farmers. The Mpumuza came to live on the southern slopes of the mountain, no doubt taking in the Blackridge area too, John said. The Zondi were further up the Edendale valley, under Inkosi Dlaba. And the Nxamalala seem to have been near Cedara, moved by the Natal government in the late 1850s to Mpendle, to act as a buffer against Bushman raids.

So, he explained, they all came to live near Swartkop mountain at this unsettled time, probably choosing this location because of the broken Mistbelt country with its substantial areas of forest to hide out in. They kept as low a profile as they could when the Boers arrived in the late 1830s and proceeded to lay out the grid of roads and properties that designated the place they named Pietermaritzburg. In the years that followed, the resident black farmers succeeded to some extent in retaining use of the land, if not on their own terms. Once the region came under British rule as part of the Colony of Natal, the first so-called native location that the Natal government proclaimed was the large tract of land in the valley beyond the Ridge which they called the Swartkop Location. It was 1846, and the Mpumuza, the Zondi, and the Nxamalala were still living there. When the railway line tracked through a few decades later, two of the chiefs were magnanimously remembered by their conquerors in the naming of two minor rural stations: Dlaba Halt and Teteleku Halt.

I found a picture of Inkosi Teteleku Zondi of the Mpumuza in the Campbell Collection, a young man dressed magnificently from head to foot in layers of fleecy hides, facing the camera directly with shield and stick in hand, in front of a neatly woven grass house.[48] He is said to be 'of Zwartkop location', but there is no indication of where exactly his home was located. After John's suggestion that Mpumuza territory would no doubt have included Blackridge, I looked for more references to the chief's residence.

In the colonial visitor's guide to the territory, *Natal Province: Descriptive Guide and Official Hand-Book* of 1911, the reader is taken on an imagniary tour of the region by railway, and the narrator pauses at Zwaartkop station, which became Blackridge station. Here he points out not only the chief's kraal, but also the school my grandmother had attended ten years before as a boarder from Dundee:

> A point of interest is Teteleku's kraal, which is only one mile from the village and is on the hill overlooking the railway line. It is now in possession of Chief Laduma, son of the late Teteleku and the natives in the district are under him. Near the station is the Uplands High School, which is a popular seminary for girls.[49]

One account places the homestead just over the crest of the Ridge, overlooking the Edendale valley, and a map puts it somewhere to the northwest of the station.[50] Whatever its actual coordinates, the proximity of the site to Blackridge gives a hint of the extent of possible communication between the native location and the white settlement. Every day men and women from the Swartkop side would have made their way down the hill to work, and sometimes the contact went the other way.

The chief's house was accessible by rail from Pietermaritzburg, and he had maintained sufficiently cordial relations with the colonial authorities to be counted as one of the Colony's so-called loyal chiefs. So 'Laduma's Kraal' became a congenial destination for the occasional official visit, and in 1905 it was a highpoint on the itinerary of an expedition of members of the British Association for the Advancement of Science. It is recorded that, after climbing the Ridge, the visitors spent most of the day at the site, drinking beer with the chief, sharing the feast of two oxen that the government had provided for the hundreds of people who had gathered from the surrounding area, taking photographs of exotic men and women and the *iqhugwane* (grass houses) where they lived, and buying such things as beadwork belts, a woman's hairpin, and a woman's necklet which they brought home to document and organise for display at the Pitt Rivers Museum at Oxford. In retrospect, the Swartkop visit was significant in that it provided a sort of 'collection hotspot' for subsequent British anthropology. That particular assemblage of artefacts from the chief's homestead, together with the artefacts of its classification and organisation, was to help define how museum collections were set up in the future, and to promote influential notions of tribal identity, specifically the idea of being 'Zulu'.[51]

Inevitably then, the pictures I could find of Laduma's vanished house appeared through a distorted lens. Yet even so, the glimpse they offered of the intricate life of the place brought home to me how close, geographically at least, those *iqhugwane* were to the wood-and-iron houses of the little white settlement they called Blackridge. Just over the railway line at the top of the hill.

I opened up Google again to look as closely as I could – from my desk in Cape Town – at the territory on the other side of the Ridge, where Mpumuza is now one neighbourhood in the sprawling Vulindlela district. Once proclaimed by the colonial masters as the first-ever native location, and later designated by the apartheid masters as a piece of the home-land of KwaZulu, the region on the other side was meant to be another country. The street view on my laptop showed a realm of rondavels and small rectangular houses in the valley, roofs made of corrugated iron held down by stones, a dry place whose contours held the memory of farming, a land of small roads and paths that meandered into the world like the branches of trees, or the course of rivers, or veins on the back of the hand. Twenty-something years after the end of apartheid, the place was still in a sense a world apart, where even Google Maps didn't know the names of the roads. Again and again I would zoom in to a particular place photographed by the all-seeing and sightless eye of the Google camera, and be given the location simply as 'unnamed road'. Unnamed road, Mpumuza. Unnamed road, Komkhulu. Unnamed road, Sweetwaters.

If I wanted more, I'd have to visit the actual place, meet real people, listen to their stories. But after all, there was no need for further evi-dence. Whatever legitimacy it may or may not have had, the undocu-mented event known as the Blackridge land invasion carried with it the burden of an unrelenting history. I imagined people from Caluza or Nenzokuhle encamped under plastic sheeting, the municipality moving them off, propertied residents meeting to discuss appropriate action, de-velopers checking out the land for townhouses …

By this point my research into my mother's particular home really had all come to a dead end, and now the long long story of invasion and dispossession in the area was simply drowning out the private ur-gencies of our specific narrative. It was time to let it go.

And then I sang the lullaby with Joseph.

It was Sazi Dlamini's idea. A musician and ethnomusicologist from Durban, he had said I should ask Joseph. That he would know it, if any-one did.

'Joseph?'

'Shabalala.'

'Of course. Ladysmith Black Mambazo.'

When I called Sazi at a friend's suggestion we somehow found ourselves talking about the *Amdokwe* chant, which he also remembered from listening to Radio Bantu in the sixties. We were the same age, and the sound of it was inscribed in both our memories, inseparable from the call of that particular bird.

'It's *ivukuthu*,' he said. 'The dove.'

'They used to play it on Radio Bantu when I was a child.'

'Yes!' he remembered. 'It was the children's programme. Nine thirty in the morning.'

He started making the dove's call, hooting through his hands into the phone.

'Sounds really do take you *right* back into the memory,' I said.

'Yes, it's very direct.'

So Sazi knew *Amdokwe*, but he couldn't translate my mother's lullaby. All I knew of the meaning was that somehow the song concluded with the sound of cannons on the Ladysmith mountain, guns from Alan Smallie's war. It was frightening, yes, but seemed to make a kind of sense. For do we not find some of the most beautiful lullabies unsettling, even as we are held in the arms of our mother's song?

I got Joseph Shabalala's number from his agent, and told him the story. I said I was looking for the words of the lullaby my mother used to sing me, that it was the one she herself had had as a child in Natal, that she was now very old and remembered only the earliest things, and that I wanted to be able to sing it with her again, and to understand the words. I explained that I felt shy to sing it to him because the song had been repeated so often that its meaning was probably lost.

'Yes, repetition. That is lullaby.' His voice was gentle. 'Hold on,' he said, 'I want to take a pen. I'm very serious about this.'

Tentatively, I sang the words I knew. I was in Cape Town and he was in Durban. He listened and asked me to sing it again. The second time he began to join in with a harmony.

'I know it!' he said, and sang the song once more, working out the words. 'It's from the early times. They would sing it at a wedding. It's an apology. It says we are not fighting, we were not quarrelling. It's a calling to forgive one another.'

166

'Wow.'

'When you come with this, you are extending things. I'm just back from America where we have been recording lullabies for three months. I think this is the time for raising up everything which is falling down. Watering the seeds.'

We sang it again together, harmonising.

'It's saying, dear lady, we are not fighting.'

'Would it be for the man or the lady to sing?'

'It's for everybody.'

'And the cannons, *mbayimbayi*?'

'They remind us of the day when we love one another. We say that to love one another . . . We say I love you like something that shoots me.'

'So you mean that the cannon, which is about wars and violence, the sound of those cannons on Mbulwana during the Siege of Ladysmith . . . You are saying that in the song the cannon has become something to do with love?'

'Yes! When we say this, *kwaduma mbayimbayi*, we say this when we love one another. The love is so powerful, it is like a thundering. I've used that part about *mbayimbayi*,' he said, and sang his version in a warm tenor voice.

'But now you came with something,' he went on generously. 'We must be sure I have your number and your name.'

'Joseph, this is wonderful. This song has been with me all my life, my mother's lullaby, but I never really understood it.'

'Yes, it is wonderful. Call me anytime.'

'And the song, it was for weddings, but it could also be a lullaby?'

'Wedding, lullaby, it fits everywhere.'

'Thank you, Joseph. Now I can sing it with her.'

It was, as he put it, a song that was singing in the early time. We sang it again together over the telephone:

> *Sasingaxabene*
> *Wemsheli wam*
> *Kwaduma mbayimbayi*

167

Phansi kwembulwane.

Afterwards, I called my friend Abner Nyamende at UCT, and together we came up with this translation:[52]

> We had not quarrelled
> My beloved
> The cannon was thundering
> Below Mbulwana.

15.

'Sometimes the sky looks lovely,' she told me. 'And sometimes the clouds have been just pulled apart. You can hear it. That's when you forget things.'

Each day, clarity and confusion, happiness and anguish washed through her room. I made the skirt at last from a piece of hand-printed cotton, and she was glad. But when I brought a notebook to leave at the bedside and wrote in it the family tree she'd asked for, it made her sad and she called it 'the book with all the d's in it'. Hoping, I suppose, to fix her days into the linear sequence of historical time, and to help her remember our visits, I had given her a diary. But one of the nurses wrote her own shopping lists across several of the weeks, and the next time I visited, a chunk of pages had been torn out. After a while the diary disappeared completely, along with certain other things. It's endemic in nursing homes, people told me. Things go missing. Many things.

So as the winds began to chill and the year slipped towards winter, the leaves of the syringa tree turned yellow before they fell, and the rhythm of her hours was tracked in the pulse of clouds. Sometimes the sky was lovely. And sometimes, when the clouds had been pulled apart, she felt lonely again, bereft of stories, cut adrift from a lifetime of memory. As the unravelling continued, she became more and more explicit about the pain of it.

After two nights out of town, I returned to a particularly cross and distressed call: 'Please say your prayers tonight and ask that I should die tonight.'

'What?'

'I'm so desperately lonely.'

Then she explained that Mrs D had told the nurses they would lose their jobs if they fed the pigeons.

'I thought . . . these people are wicked,' she said, hugely upset. 'They think the old people are just things, no real consciousness.'

I wanted to call management right away, but I was so angry that I didn't feel I could trust myself to handle it properly. Instead I promised to ask the doctor to write them a letter saying the birds were essential for her mental health.

She was glad of that, but the distress would not subside: 'You can't *imagine* what it's like.'

'No I can't. But I am trying.'

'Well I feel like a *swine*.'

'You're not a swine. We all just have to try and muddle along.'

'Well you're muddling along with a *family* all around you.'

'I can't help that. You felt quite happy when we came to see you on Monday.'

'That was because *you* were there.'

'Well I can't *live* there.'

'I know you can't.'

For the hundredth time, I wondered what alternative there was. Couldn't she come and live with us? Not really. It was excruciating.

The next time she said something similar, I went to visit straight away.

'You obviously don't care tuppence about me,' she had told me on the phone. 'Just pray. Ask God that I can die.'

I felt washed out. Just sat with her. I told her about my friend who had just died from cancer. He had a young wife and babies, and didn't want to die. But he had. Now she was old, and wanted to die, but was still alive. We both cried.

'I realise that I'm always trying to fix things, make it better,' I said. 'But I just can't fix this. I can't make it better.'

We were quiet together then. I realised how often my approach with her had been to avoid facing the pain. Try to cheer her up. This time when I left, there was a kind of peace.

'What a lovely visit,' she said.

Over weeks and months, the themes of her distress repeated themselves with utter clarity. And a lifetime of 'speaking her mind' and a love of poetic imagery combined with whatever changes were taking place in her brain to make for a mercilessly direct take on her situation.

'For extreme cruelty, I suggest you spend a night here,' she told me one morning. 'Absolute cut-off. However, never mind . . . They're angry with the whites. But I suppose you could say we asked for it.'

The door opened and a male nurse brought her coffee. He was a black African man, very friendly. She greeted him with a smile.

Another time she told me, 'I'm tired of this place. No friendliness. I don't know anybody who's got any liveliness in them. It's like a rubbish heap where old people are chucked . . . The trees are having a wonderful time today against an *incredible* blue sky.'

And then, almost conversationally, she added, 'It's a terrible thing.'

'What is?'

'To lose your personality.'

From the outside, she seemed not to have lost her personality at all. But what then was lost? And what remained? Anguish and despair, the sadness of it, rested in the heart like a great seabird weighed down by black oil. But right in the midst, she would remember joy. It seemed as ineradicable as weeds or sunlight.

'I'm *so* miserable,' she told me one morning. 'But then I look at the green, and I look at the green. It *is* beautiful. The garden is the main thing here.'

'I think you would go mad if you lived in a place without a garden.'

'Oh I'm so glad you said *go* mad. I thought I'd already gone. Maybe I went and came back.'

On Mother's Day we arrived with daffodils and treats, and she said delightedly, 'I've never heard of Mother's Day before.'

'You have.'

'I have not!'

We all laughed.

'Oh goodness me!' she said. 'I suddenly felt full of gladness. It's a physical thing.'

'It's called serotonin,' Sky said.

But already she was watching the squirrel on the syringa branch.

'They get away with a lot,' she said. 'They're so charming.'

A while back she had told us that, if you look carefully, you'll notice that squirrels move about in a sinister way.

'You still think it looks sinister?' Sophie asked.

'No. But if you see it crawling along quietly . . .'

The twins put out grain for the pigeons and suddenly the flock all appeared on the verandah.

'Look!' she said. 'They just grow out of the ground. Look at their heads, pecking the grains. They look just like engines. They think it's Christmas now. He's a real bully that one . . . he's terrible. Not a very nice bird.'

From the courtyard below, little old Mrs D also appeared on cue, shaking her finger at the children with a fierce expression: 'Don't feed the pigeons!'

'Just ignore her,' I told them. 'I know she looks like the old witch in a fairy story, but we've got the doctor's letter.'

Then Granny made us laugh again by telling the story of the Friday fish.

'The other day a nurse brought my lunch with a fish laid out flat on the plate. As she put the plate down, she pointed to it and told me in a very firm voice, "*I* will eat that fish." I said, "Yes, you will eat it." And she did. Not a nice thing to look at. It's funny . . . If a thing is funny it brings a haze of other feelings with it. Some people would be shocked. I wonder what she would have done if I'd said no. But nothing looked worse than that fish. It was so thoroughly dead, stretched across in a languid position taking up most of the plate. This food is very bad, I think. Very awful.'

As we were leaving, she said, 'Barts and Letty were my favourite people in the family. We used to fight, you and I.'

'No we didn't, because I'm your daughter.'

'I think you must write it up on your forehead.'

16.

She could still make us laugh, and often did. Or smile. And she could still reflect on her own condition.

'I'm always very tired,' she told me on the phone. 'Boredom, I suppose, is one of the things.'

'You sound out of breath.'

'Oh I'm out of *everything!*' And then she went on, 'That's such a lovely window. The *waving* line of the branches, and the little criss-cross.'

Long after she'd given up trying to draw or sew, she still wrote small poems, and her capacity for observation took in the syringa tree, the birds and squirrels, the nursing home staff, the details of things in the landscape of her room, and the ever-changing currents of her own mind. Across her TV screen, stuck in place on her instruction, was an enlarged photograph of the patch of Mistbelt forest growing below the old station, near Graham Tegg's house at Blackridge. She had no interest in television but loved to gaze at the picture, and to hear how the railway line was now gone, supplanted.

'It's released from being civilised!' she said on one visit. 'Lovely. So things can grow.'

When I reminded her about the monkey we'd seen there, she beamed.

'Oh it's lovely for monkeys. Planted especially for monkeys.'

The affinity with living things that she'd felt since childhood, and her capacity for awareness, meant she was especially attuned to the plants that appeared in her immediate environment. In a sense their condition was like a mirror of her own. So while she'd been glad to see the ferns I brought back, after a while they began to concern her.

'This fern looks like Dad when he was in a bad temper,' she told me one day. 'He used to rattle off swear words. It didn't worry me at all. It worried Mother of course. Seventeenth essence of damn pig!'

Then on Midwinter's Day she said very emphatically, 'Those plants ought to be out in the garden, in the fresh air. It's cruel to keep them in pots. If I was a plant, I wouldn't like it.'

'You always want things to be free. Children too.'

'I think that's right. And trees chopped down. I hate to hear of a tree chopped down.'

I said I'd take the ferns home, and she was grateful.

'They'll *spread*. If Mother doesn't want the plants, will you have them? I'd like to see them out in the sun.'

'You know,' she went on, 'I was trying to say funeral, and I said celebration.'

'I suppose a funeral can be a kind of celebration.'

'Yes it should be.'

I tied up the net curtains that cut off the view through the side window, and she said, 'What wonderful things you can do with curtains! Look at the sun through that red cloth. Lovely.'

The next plants to go were the artificial flowers, nursing home décor.

'I'm so tired of that vase of artificial flowers,' she told me. 'And they last forever! You can't even throw them away. They don't even die.'

I said something about the flowers being like trying to fix impermanence. You wish there was something to hold on to, something that can't disintegrate. But real flowers are beautiful, and they die.

'Yes,' she said. 'Lives are beautiful, and they pass on. But these flowers, it's interfering with the pattern, with the movement. They interfere with the movement of what happens. The real ones are performing correctly in the movement.'

'Well we can just get rid of them.'

'Oh would you? They take a lot of looking at. Give them to someone who might like them.'

We talked about trying to hold on to things. Not wanting to die.

She said, 'If people don't agree to move on, there's a hold-up of the whole development. Those other real flowers that someone gave me, they're wonderful. They enjoy being alive. Oh darling, tell me not to be sorry for myself.'

'Be like those flowers.'

'You've got to be strong and full of life,' she said. 'Well not really. You've got to realise that you're part of a development, the development of human beings, the changes that they go through. Some are good and cheerful, like those plants, and some wither and drag about and trip people up. I've got a feeling of a road in my mind, a road that people have to go on, whether they like it or not. In fact I think that's a silly thing. In fact we create our direction.'

'So what should we do?'

'We can stand up and direct, decide where to go.'

A fake-sounding voice came through with some instructions on the intercom. We both laughed.

'The staff are actually quite nice here,' she said. 'And those rusks you brought me . . . You offer the nurses a rusk, and just watch them light up.'

17.

Once I'd stopped trying to find the house, it was easy to slip into my mother's sense of immediacy in which the nursing home room and its garden filled up the present moment and Blackridge took form as a mythic realm rather than an actual place. But every now and then an email would come in from Francois that reminded me.

In late July, he wrote, 'The mountain is very drab and grey. The grass has been burnt on a number of occasions. Nothing has come of the land invasion I told you earlier about. In the meantime I noticed an application to develop an area at the end of Albany Road. Talking of the Mistbelt: the area above Albany Road is known to have Hilton daisies (*Gerbera aurantiaca*) which only come out if the grass has been burnt. They are red and look like the Barberton daisies. This is just below the Mistbelt. Your mum would be able to remember something of that.'

She used to love Barberton daisies, so I was sure she'd remember a Hilton daisy. But she'd need to see it. Her response to the name was vague.

'They grow old,' she said.

'What do?'

'The memories.'

For a while we'd been talking about memory itself. I thought it might be comforting to suggest that the erosion of her memories was a medical condition, rather than being in any sense her fault. So we'd found ourselves speaking about the brain, a subject that neither of us knew anything about.

'Brains are funny things,' she said one morning. 'They get all tangled up.'

She'd been telling me about a dream in which she wanted to leave the nursing home and go to Blackridge. Now on waking (pigeons on the verandah, dappled sunlight, big trees) she found the dream strange.

'I like it here,' she said. But then, 'The word "cling" comes to mind. Why do we cling to past places? Or cling to pictures of past places?'

'Why do you think?'

She laughed. 'I don't know! The word "ferocious" comes to mind. I feel ferocious towards anyone who says those places don't matter. It sounds like a wild animal.'

'And why do those places matter?'

'Perhaps because one was very much alive there.'

'You sometimes say such bizarre things, but otherwise you're still so wise and clear.'

'Why is that?'

'Different parts of the brain, maybe. Some are fine. Others have begun to atrophy.'

'Atrophy. A marvellous word. Sort of dusty.'

I explained as best I could what I'd been reading about the hippocampus in relation to other parts of the brain. That the shrinking of the hippocampus can mean it's difficult to form new memories, while your oldest memories may still be intact.

'Once you get that into your mind, you don't feel so responsible,' she said. 'But what is the mind, then? I think mind is the working part – and that's certainly very busy.'

I said, 'I think it's difficult if the mind is working okay, but its building blocks, the memories, get faulty. So sometimes you sound very clear, but you're using faulty memory blocks.'

She was concentrating, thinking hard. 'There may be a reason for your mind to *forget* something you don't want to remember. If it's a thing you can't handle, you put it away and you forget it as though it didn't happen.'

'I suppose we all do that.'

'It's fascinating . . . They try to upset what you want to believe now. You don't want to be reminded.'

'What things?'

'Well (I'm making this up . . .), perhaps something you did, and you try to wash it away as though it didn't happen.'

'Do you do that?'

'I think we do it all the time. Our frontal part can't handle too many things at once.'

It was early morning, she'd just eaten a few bites of the awful nursing home breakfast, and we were talking about consciousness and repression. I mentioned the book *My Stroke of Insight*, a brain scientist's story of her own transformative experience of stroke. My mother said she'd like to read it.

Next, we tried thinking about memory as a sequence of layers, like the stratigraphy in an archaeological dig. The paradox of archaeological excavation is that, in order to perceive what's there, you must destroy the record: dig up the site. But with memory it seems that the act of remembering both fixes the memory and also, in a sense, creates it. So in this case, the paradox is that if you don't revisit the memory through repetition, it may be gone forever.

Still, there could be a sense in which looking for Blackridge was like visiting an archaeological site: a search for something hidden in the dark, the ash floor beneath. When the hippocampus is damaged and short-term memories become inaccessible, it's as though the upper layers of the site have been destroyed. But the very early ones are still somewhat available, like the deepest levels of the dig.

I wrote a quick list of key stages in her life, sequenced from last down to first like the layers of an excavation: Cape Town, retirement, Epworth, mother (Julie), married (Mick), Adams College, England, school, Blackridge.

'Yes,' she said, 'and some of the things that happen never reappear. You can't control it. They seem to have a power of their own that you are independent of. Do you think that's possible? It's like a postbox (I can understand something if I can see it). Some things go in and are left there. And one can say something that might stir them awake, and they gradually crawl their way out. Or they may *suddenly* shoot out. Or perhaps you never remember ... "Familiar" is a very useful word. It means to me, "yes this is true". The idea of a family.'

Familiar – truth – family. Sometimes it was the gift of the dementia to free her words for creative slippage. And sometimes the reduced inhibitions of her condition took her right into the emotional heart of the unspoken.

'A sad thing is that I haven't got warm, comfortable feelings about my mother,' she went on. 'It's quite important, really. Maybe it was different for the others. Perhaps by the time I came she was worn out. Her own mother had died. She didn't know her.'

'At least you are so aware of it, so honest.'

'Yes, what else? You look at it. You turn the page.'

Another day, talking about memory again, she told me, 'I can't stop thinking of imagined writing. I don't write it down (I'm too lazy). I seem to live in a bookshop.'

'You say things and then forget them straight away. Like clouds appearing and disappearing.'

'Like winds in the sky. I imagine I have a writing desk and I write and put things away and they just . . . disappear. I looked out of the window and thought, Chagall made that picture. The sunlight just beginning, and the dark Chagall shapes.'

'Why do you love Chagall so much?'

'Because for such a long time I hated him. He's a very expressive painter. I'm trying to imagine blobbing on paint like he does.'

'You said there were lots of imagined things in your head.'

'They don't belong to me, I'm afraid. They just come when they feel like it. No good trying to find them.'

'Are they stories?'

'Hmm. Memories.'

She was beginning to sound vague, losing the thread.

'You do like Chagall, though.'

'You have to wait to be invited into his house. And then you think, *Oh* I know what he's meaning.'

18.

I decided it was time to burn some of her papers that I'd been storing in our garage. None were precious or administratively important, just a heap of old medical bills, medical aid forms, and sundry printouts.

Sky and I made a fire in the hearth and fed them in one by one, talking about his granny. As we were doing so, a note in her handwriting caught my eye. It was a list of questions for the committee of the retirement complex where she had lived just before moving to the nursing home. She wanted to know to whom they were accountable, how they made decisions, what role the residents played, and so on.

'Look at this,' I showed him. 'It's so clear and firm.'

Together with the set of questions was a typed letter she'd circulated at about the same time to other residents in response to a groundswell of disquiet about the role of the committee in the sudden resignation of the much-loved manager. She begins with an analysis of the authoritarian tone of the committee's letters to the residents, and then goes on:

> We all have to go through many rites of passage – the first day at school, the first job. We all have to shed the known and go into the frightening unknown. To accept the fact that we are no longer able to make our own decisions, and have to move into 'protected' retirement is one of the hardest. We tend to blame our frustrations and anxieties on the people who manage our new environment. Add to this that the complex, beautiful as it is, has an unusual lot of 'teething' troubles, many of which are recurring. With the best will in the world the managers cannot control the process of restoration, let alone speed it up. But what they do, with unbelievable patience and consideration and kindness, is to

smooth the rite of passage into old age. Which is after all the most important thing they do.

As I read the letter aloud, it reminded me of a crucial part of the story: the fact that her condition of so-called dementia was not a slow vague drift into forgetfulness, or an ordinary case of Alzheimer's disease. By her mid-eighties my mother was old but lucid, wise, and engaged, and she was drawing on a lifetime of experience to think carefully about the experience of ageing. And then, quite suddenly and unexpectedly, she slid over the falls.

What changed everything was the hip operation.

One day just before Christmas she went into surgery for a hip replacement, a procedure she'd been led to believe would transform her life. It did. When she woke up from the anaesthetic she was lost and terrified.

'I'm going to lose my home!' she cried, as I walked into the ward. 'They want to take my home away! They want to turn me out! You must stop them! You have to stop them!'.

I was confused by her uncharacteristic desperation, but tried to reassure her. 'No really it's fine. You're just here in hospital for a bit, and then you're going back to your flat.'

But as the days passed, her post-operative condition became increasingly strange and frightened. Raving and dreamlike, her state of mind was unlike anything I'd known of her before. Mostly she remembered who I was, but everything else was shifting and confused. People told me this is what sometimes happens when old people are given a general anaesthetic. Nobody had mentioned it as a possibility before the operation, but afterwards there were many stories. Most often, they said, the person returns to her senses fairly soon. But after the surgery my mother never quite regained her clarity of mind.

Or perhaps it was the succession of operations that followed.

She returned to the flat in the retirement complex, was visited regularly by a physiotherapist who gave her exercises she didn't want to do, and was supervised day and night by women who sat watching television as often as they could. She told me she found them patronising, and that she hated having another person in her space all the time. But I reassured her that it would pass, and in time it did. The carers did in fact leave.

Then very early one morning her new hip dislocated. The pain was excruciating. After about four hours, when she felt sure I'd be awake, she telephoned me. I called an ambulance which took her back to hospital where she was X-rayed and anaesthetised again in order to reposition the steel ball into its socket. Afterwards, the confusion came back, and so did the carers. A few weeks later, the hip dislocated again, involving more pain, more hospital, more disorientation. The orthopaedic surgeon met with me and explained that he must do a second operation. This time, he promised to fit something that could never dislocate. So more surgery followed, more hospital, more anaesthetics, more pills. Afterwards she was crazy confused again, but also very ill, plagued by involuntary jerks. They transferred her to the hospice where she lay quite silently, with eyes closed and tongue black, and we were sure she was at the brink of death.

Then one evening Sophie said to her, 'Granny, open your eyes.'

She came back.

As a temporary measure while my mother recovered, I moved her to a nursing home where she would have twenty-four-hour care. She was thin and very frail, but brave and alive. She was learning to walk again. Then once again, the hip dislocated and she lost her bearings.

Altogether she endured seven dislocations and seven general anaesthetics.

After the seventh episode I became, for the first time, quite calm. There would be no more surgery, no more anaesthetics, I told the surgeon. I explained that she had given up trying to walk some time back, and that from now on we'd function without him. She would have a wheelchair to get around, and in bed she'd have to lie with the sky-blue cushion between her legs to prevent them from crossing. He seemed relieved to be out of the loop.

At some point during these painful months, the temporary bed in the nursing home became permanent, and I packed up her flat in the retirement complex, weeping while an old gramophone record of Beethoven's

Pastoral Symphony – her favourite, still on the turntable – played on repeat. In Frail Care the best option was the upstairs room with a little verandah and a view of the syringa tree. We moved a few familiar books, some pictures, and a little furniture into it, but by this time she no longer had the stability of mind to settle.

It was precisely the thing she'd feared: to be turned out of home. Now, when I read for the first time her earlier letter to the management about the rite of passage into old age, I realised even more acutely what she had lost in the move.

The other document I discovered and saved from the fire was from another life, but her voice was unmistakable. In an article written in 1952 for the Ramblers newsletter, a thirty-four-year-old Elizabeth Martin described the ascent of Champagne Castle in the Drakensberg:

> You see, mountains do things to you mentally. They take out every ounce of pride and patronage, and reduce your spirit to a slow animal desire to reach the next cairn, so that you will be allowed to still for a moment the banging in your head, get your heart back to its proper place, undo your ribs which are busy plaiting themselves, and get just a breath or two of air into your aching lungs. Your thoughts and your hopes and your whole being concentrate on this. It is a lot of nonsense to talk about panoramic views.[53]

And then at the summit, ecstatically:

> If you are not very fond of naartjies, little green ones, that is, steal some late at night and carry them to the top of Champagne, lie with your toes touching the beacon and get the sun to break through the mist warmly, as you peel them. Nothing in this world will taste quite so good, and thereafter they will be your favourite fruit.[54]

I sent the whole piece to Francois Marais who was, by curious coincidence, the current chairperson of the Ramblers. He wrote back to say he was including it in the next newsletter, along with a tribute to my mother and to her climbing friend Joan Reed, who had been the driving force in that particular expedition up the mountain and was now the Ramblers' oldest member.

The remainder of the documents needed burning, and as the heap of bills and forms were consigned to ash I felt a sort of lightening.

Once they were done, I began to excavate the rest of the garage.

Along with a few of her things that had been stored there since I packed up her flat in the retirement complex, there was also a great accumulation of random family possessions: wood piles, car stuff, paintings, picture frames, a messy family archive including my paternal grandfather's memoirs, my father's voice on reel-to-reel tapes, my grandmother's ostrich feather fan, a box of ancestral mother-of-pearl-handled fruit knives and forks, storybooks from three childhoods, heaps of finely illustrated schoolbooks from primary school at Waldorf, several handmade books, handmade toys, Sophie's years of journals, many drawings, a patched old kelim, two black bags of toys shoved out of the twins' rooms but not quite relinquished, a wetsuit, boogie boards, speakers and two dubious sound systems, leaves and dust blown in from the world . . . I had for so long been so absorbed in the ecosystem of the nursing home that I'd not really noticed the extent of this assemblage until it had reached the point where you couldn't drive into the garage without the possibility of crushing something.

Sorting through it all and clearing things out was, as they say, therapeutic. Water had leaked into one of the bags of toys so Pinocchio's wooden body was black with mould, the little bells that used to hang around the twins' cot had rusted, and the blue bird that Michael once sewed for Jason, his firstborn, was almost unrecognisable. I worked at the garage over weekends whenever I could, getting dirty, unearthing forgotten stories, turfing out and passing on heaps of stuff, giving the mother-of-pearl cutlery to Michael to make into jewellery, and packing a few things into storage.

As regards my mother's life before she moved to the nursing home, the garage offered several gifts, among them her fabulous collection of silks and fine patchwork materials which I absorbed into my own fabric cupboard, and the family's remaining assortment of Royal Doulton.

When I'd packed up her flat several years before, I passed on most of the things she didn't need, including the crockery, but I did wrap up a few pieces of china for some time in the future. Now that time had come, and as I peeled off the old newspapers from an accumulation of dinner plates, side plates, and other tableware from my childhood, I discovered what I was unable to admit to myself at the time when I was dismantling her home. I didn't really like it.

Royal Doulton sounds splendid, and my father with his low-key royalist inclinations enjoyed the resonance of the name. But in this case, the china is bland. First, we had Desert Star, manufactured soon after World War II, the vessels cream-coloured, sometimes rimmed with grey-green, and the design of a pale brown 'atomic' star at the centre. Then came Morning Star, which dates from the late seventies. It was a more mod version of the earlier set, the plates made of fine china, high-fired for extra durability, and glazed bright white with a spikier central star and a fine zig-zag rim.

Was it churlish not to love them? The plates and bowls might be retro now, but few people whom I know of my generation enjoy the mainstream aesthetic of those years. Or maybe it was the food, the quotidian meals. Or simply the fact that daily crockery is so intimate. For whatever reason, as I unpacked the plates and bowls we had used each day, they seemed to summon from the past a particular ambience of white English-speaking middle-class family life in a provincial city in South Africa in the sixties and seventies. Something of that era had become inscribed in the very china. It was something airless and heavy, even if your parents were creative people with liberal values.

I packed them up again, to give away.

Then one day I noticed that the Blackridge ferns and the little oak sapling from the Hoek had taken root in our garden, and that other plants had germinated in the red clay soil I'd brought with them from beside the old railway platform.

Like the practical work of clearing out the garage, the process of identifying them and tracking their trajectories on the global botanical map was a quiet relief from the emotional intensities of the nursing home. The fluffy blue *Ageratum houstonianum*, or Cope's Folly, turned out to be native to Mexico and Central America, a Category 1 declared weed. The wild violets, *Centella asiatica*, were indigenous to Africa and parts of Asia, and traditionally used as a medicinal herb in KwaZulu-Natal. The tiny mushrooms were bird's nest fungi, *Cyathus olla*, that grow across the world from Europe to South America to Australia. And the violet morning glory, *Ipomea indica,* that came climbing up to peer into my study window was another plant from Mexico and Central America. It was a Category 1 declared weed in KwaZulu-Natal, but a slightly less serious Category 3 plant in the Western Cape.

What to do? My mother's instruction to bring back something growing had opened the door. I let them all flower, and pulled up the invasive aliens before they could set seed.

19.

At some time during what was to be my mother's last spring, my grandmother Madge Smallie née Tatham finally died.

We were going through the usual cycle of questions and answers about her death when my mother suddenly said, 'Oh, I can remember her funeral! I don't remember her actually dying, but I can remember standing at the graveside. The grave had been dug very neatly, quite perfectly really. I said to myself, Mother would have approved of that.'

Once the memory of the neatly dug grave came to the surface, the stories of Mother began to fade away. And after a while she was gone, released completely into the past. Of her own death, my mother began to speak quite often, sometimes in utter desperation and sometimes with a sense of equanimity.

Often, she would say, 'I'm tired of being me.'

Then one day she told me, 'This place is . . . I'm trying to find the right word for lonely. I just want to go Home now. I don't mean 'home' with a small 'h'. I mean the great Home. But God obviously doesn't want me.'

When I said nothing, she went on, 'The loneliness is *unbelievable*. I didn't think it was *possible*.'

'It's a sort of isolation.'

'Isolation, yes. As though I've done something wrong.'

'Well you really haven't done anything wrong. And I do come and see you, but you don't remember . . . And Lyle does too.'

Lyle was her best friend, the gentle priest for whom she used to make brightly embroidered vestments. At her funeral, he walked down the aisle showing everyone the flames and the phoenix that he was wearing, the bright leaves and flowers she had stitched in silk.

'Give him my best love,' she said. 'After you. You are my best love, but after you. *Lots* of love, darling. *All that I've got.*'

Perhaps my quest was simply a testament of love. Like the lullaby from my grandfather's War. Love that is like a thundering. That is inextricable from the recognition of death.

One morning when I visited her she told me, 'There's a moaning wind outside.'

'What is it moaning about?'

'It doesn't want to be a wind any more.'

'What does it want to be?'

'It wants to be a wave . . . I want to be a wave.'

Another time she said, 'I am enjoying, really, being near to death, as they say. It's very quiet and peaceful. And everything is all right.'

On one such tender morning she looked up as I appeared at her bedside, and said, 'I must have dreamed you here. I called you in a dream.'

She had been gazing at the light in the leaves of the syringa tree.

'That waving branch,' she pointed. 'The squirrels love it. It was made for them, I think. They just sort of melt along. Funnily enough, when they go along that branch, they look a little bit sinister. It's odd, because squirrels are not sinister.'

Once again, she couldn't remember that I was her daughter. Couldn't really believe it. In the beginning, it used to worry me, but now it no longer seemed important. We both laughed.

'You were a teacher too, you know. A special one. You got children to make plays and art and poetry. You really believed in it. In us. I was there too. We used to make all sorts of things, and we'd paint on the walls, and use hot wax and sharp tools, and you'd put on Bach and Beethoven while we worked. Sometimes we did movement to music. You didn't care about following the timetable, and you never minded if we made a mess.'

'I was a teacher?'

She looked amazed.

'I think you still are. But it's strange, isn't it, how these memories drift.'

'Yes, it seems a pity.'

She sat for a while, watching the light in the tree, and then went on to tell me about an old man she'd known for a long time.

'I understand some sort of monk person, a little man, old, sitting on a hill, and watching people go past. Not just walking past, but *living* past. He wasn't an ordinary human being. He was a sort of spirit, and he was replaying the years that are gone.'

'That's a nice image.'

'He replayed the years that were gone. Yes, it's coming clear now. Somehow, he was given this gift, to watch the development of people. And he watched the people growing through the various stages of their lives, from their youth to where they ended.'

'You know,' she said, laughing, 'I've got double vision. When I look at that pigeon I see two of them.'

'And what are you doing in the story of the old man?'

'I was just noticing him. I wasn't in the story, but perhaps we were sort of conscious of him, someone told us about him. He's there all the time, you know, *watching*. And he's not affected by the human idea of good and bad. He has a spiritual idea, and he knows *exactly*. He watches . . . This particular man who has now grown old. He has watched his path and he knows that he's come to the end of it.'

'And where are you?'

'I just . . . have been told about that old man. I know what started it, I was thinking about Dad and Mr Gilchrist. He was a kind old man, and he was very anxious about my spiritual development. I think I told you he gave me stories. Stories out of the Bible, and a Christian newspaper for children. I didn't know there was such a thing.'

'And it was because of Mr Gilchrist that your family left Blackridge.'

Somehow it was Mr Gilchrist who led to them all being evicted from the Garden.

'Yes, he was said to be in some sort of trouble at the Tech. There was a lot of quarrelling, and my father signed off and went home.'

Then she said, 'The old man watching. That's right.'

'It's a powerful image.'

'It goes *right* back. I'm sure there was a Mr Gilchrist, a little man with

189

very white hair. Very gentle, but very definite in what he thought. And Dad . . . he had great affection, great sympathy. His bits don't mix together: careless soldier, excited, and then a return to reality, dull and dismal. He was a wonderful man, really, really, really.'

We talked about other things, then. The terrible breakfast, the birds, the signs of spring in the syringa tree. Stuck across her television screen, the picture of the glade of forest at Blackridge was a portal into that untrammelled place where creepers climb high into the trees, the summer grasses are alive with butterflies, and baby bats sleep in the banana leaves. The place in the mind where the railway used to be was wild again.

'We used to walk along the railway line and pick wild flowers,' she said. 'There was a steep bank on either side.'

'Do you remember Hilton daisies?'

'That rings a bell. Yellow? I just remember flowers. We didn't think of names for them.'

20.

'So do you want me to prescribe an antibiotic? It's pneumonia.'

I was driving when the doctor phoned. I said I'd think about it and call back.

My parents had signed a living will many years before, and my mother had been talking about death for some time. Now she was coughing, and I found myself repeating stock phrases I'd heard from other people: we don't want to prolong her life unnaturally, we want her to be comfortable. And so on. Still, it was difficult and sad and confusing.

Then I spoke to the twins and they made the obvious suggestion: 'Ask Granny.'

My mother's response was unambiguous.

'Of *course* I want to get better.'

So we sent for the antibiotic.

Over the next while the cough cleared, mostly. But she had passed through a certain threshold.

Before the coughing started she'd said to me, 'I'm in the process of giving up.'

'Giving up on what?'

'On being. I've been me for a long time.'

'Are you fading?'

'Yes, very slowly. But certainly.'

'Is that good?'

'It's okay. It's what everyone will do in the end.'

Now the fading was a little more evident every day. Two weeks after the antibiotic, when the nursing home called to say she was struggling to breathe, I went straight away. As I walked up the staircase a noise that sounded like a vacuum cleaner attached to an electric drill came

191

roaring out of her room. It was the nebuliser, its mask strapped over her mouth.

She was alone, and I could just make out what she was saying, to whoever might happen to hear: 'Please take it off.'

I unclipped the mask and switched off the machine. Quiet settled in the room. It was the only thing to do.

Afterwards I had the lovely task of picking a bucket full of roses for Michael's annual jewellery exhibition. My heart hurt, but the roses were as beautiful as roses. As I picked, a black crow flew down from a perfect blue sky and sat watching me companionably.

Later in the day, Sky came with me to see her. The staff said she had stopped responding to them. Not waking up. There was no response to me either, and she looked very frail and absent in her pale nightie. But when Sky gave her a hug, she opened her eyes.

'Hello,' she said. And smiled, like the sun coming out from behind the clouds.

'Do you want the nebuliser on again?' we asked.

'I'd rather not breathe.'

Next day when both twins and I went to visit, she was back, smiling broadly to see us, her cheeks like two red apples.

'I'm so lucky to have you,' she said.

Walking afterwards along the sea to St James, we met a baby seal stranded on a rock at the edge of the path. She barked and snarled when I reached out to her, then rested her head on a rock with a look of exhaustion, or perhaps despair.

'Look, she's crying,' Sky said.

We stood watching, unable to help or to leave. Then suddenly she slipped backwards off the rock and fell. It looked painful, but the fall dislodged her. She turned her head and lifted herself up to face the water, flip-flopped across the sand, over the rocks, into the wave, and out to sea.

'Like Granny,' Sky said.

It was December, long warm days. I'd swim at Muizenberg first thing, and then go to the nursing home. Sometimes I would climb into the bed and lie with her. She'd kiss my forehead, and we'd watch the pigeons and the squirrels together. The tree was full of dappled summer leaves. Wordless hours.

In the beginning, I'd imagined that looking for the Blackridge house was like setting off into the dark forest of a fairy tale. Now it was real, her journey. In. Out. Fluid in the lungs. Thread of breath, continuing.

On Christmas Eve, she said to me, 'I don't know. That's the answer to most things.'

'What do you mean?'

'I don't know.'

I told her the Zen story in which the teacher asks a monk, 'Where are you going?'

He answers, 'Around on pilgrimage.'

The teacher says, 'What is the purpose of pilgrimage?'

The monk says, 'I don't know.'

The teacher says, 'Not knowing is nearest.'

'Yes,' my mother said. 'It's like that.'

'I wish I could take this cough away from you,' I said.

'It can't be helped.'

How things drop away under the gaze of eternity. On Christmas morning the family arrived to see her but the visit was just too much and we left with her gifts unopened. In the afternoon just the twins and I went again, and it was quiet and good. The room filled up with sadness and light. Golden chrysanthemums in a vase. Scarlet roses. Pigeons coming for food on the verandah. Kisses on her forehead, on her face, old lips kissing my cheeks. A piece of chocolate slipped into her open mouth. Dinu Lipatti playing the Schubert Impromptu in G Flat Major at his final concert. Sky showed her photographs of flowers on his iPod, and it made her smile. Then he held up a picture of a dog from the internet, and she smiled again and whispered the name of the dog she remembered: 'Ladybird.'

Some evenings later, Lyle administered the last rites. I walked in as it was happening, and her face lit up: 'Julie!'

Sophie had brought her a big crimson rose, and she loved it completely.

'Utterly beautiful,' she said.

On such an evening in deep summer, the Valley of the Shadow is no longer a dark forest but the lighted room in a nursing home, cough ripping through the night. Once the nebuliser has been turned off, each breath is audible. In. Out. In. Out. Quietness and the sounding breath. A few particular words, whispered. A smile that radiates across her whole face, creasing the wrinkles around her eyes, wrinkling up her nose.

'It's like the photographs of her as a little girl,' Sophie whispers. 'Like a baby.'

A cough rips through again, and her forehead creases. It's like watching clouds moving across the sky, like the face of a baby as the feelings form and dissolve. Once more, the wind is howling. Once more, the breath moves in and out. Another cough tears through and subsides. How things drop away.

What happens when the last breath stops?

The long days roll on. Words and stories settle into silence. The television has become a shrine, with the picture of the Blackridge wildness stuck across the screen, the branch of lichen and Sophie's little rabbit made of shells resting on the top, and an offering of red roses and golden chrysanthemums at the base. Lying in the bed with her, I put my head against her breast as I used to when I was small. Her chest is bony, heart beating loud and slowly within.

Her teaching now is quietness and the sounding breath. Not knowing is nearest. In the luminous gap between the worlds, the rose shrine is my beacon. The children have said their goodbyes.

On the last day, Sophie packs lunch for me to take to the nursing home. It is the first time she has ever done such a thing, and I can feel the generations turning over.

The day is long and warm, midsummer. The syringa tree is dappled with sunlight. Pigeons and squirrels visit the verandah. Roses gleam at the foot of the bed. Resting in the quiet space of her dying, I visit the garden where the bright old koi are so big you could hug them, wrap arms around their generous bulk and dive down slowly into the dark. Their soft fish mouths meet my fingers at the surface, nibble at the edge of the deep.

In her bed, my mother is breathing. This breath, our breath, the single thread of effort and attention that keeps her with us.

The room is quiet. Translucent. Nothing to do but what is here.

At such a time, nothing else meets the clarity of a mother's head against the pillow, cough tearing through her chest, the tough breath labouring. When she surfaces for a moment from the dream where she is travelling, her eyes open to look at me and a small smile moves the corners of her mouth.

'Hello.'

Fish swim in water clear. Pigeons jostle for food on the verandah. What gift for the living shall I bring back from the dead? This heart is a rose. This mind is a diamond. This life is sunlight. This death is the rain.

Her breath comes fast and ragged. When she's distressed, I sing the lullaby. When the twins call, I tell her they send lots of love, and her whole faces crinkles into a smile.

Things drop away. Just the sound of the breath, her breath, mucus in the lungs, difficult. Another cough rips through and subsides. Her face contracts and releases. Clouds passing across the sky.

All day the breath moves in and out, her breath and mine. What will happen when it stops?

All day there is nowhere else to be, nothing else to do. I sit beside her. Sometimes I sing the lullaby. Sometimes I reach for her hand where she lies on the white bed, breathing and sweating. The bright old koi in the garden are big enough to take me with them, arms clasped around a fish-scaled girth, diving into the deep.

All day her room is quiet, full of light. My heart hurts. It feels like birth.

THE STREAM

1.

What brought me back was a name, and the paths that led from it. It was winter again but too little rain had fallen, and my mind was full of that particular mist that comes to confuse the senses after the first flush of a mother's death.

In the tender days and weeks after she died, my refuge had been solitude. A stone sinking into the quiet of a mountain pool. We cleared out the nursing home room the afternoon before the funeral. Clothes and the TV set for the nurses, birdseed for her neighbour, wheelchair to the hospice, boxes of books and pictures to bring home.

Once that was done, I was content to do very little. It was a translucent time, and it would never come again.

At last, after nearly six months, I began to look at her remaining worldly goods, specifically the books she'd had in the nursing home at the end. The titles were familiar, their spines a defining element of the environments she'd always created, wherever she lived. The Thames and Hudson *From Giotto to Cézanne: A Concise History of Painting*, John Berger's *Success and Failure of Picasso*, the lavishly illustrated *The Tree of Life: Image for the Cosmos*. Then two volumes turned up that I didn't recognise at all. Both had belonged to my grandmother.

The first was a scholarly monograph about Rembrandt that included 159 illustrations, each discussed in detail. It seemed to be a sensitive interpretation of the work, and showed clear signs of having been read. But what made the book extraordinary for me was the insight it gave into the unrecorded life of the formidable person they called Mother. Not a single story of my grandmother had ever mentioned that she could draw, or that she cared about art history. Art was what Betty did. But stuck onto the front page of the Rembrandt book was a plaque from Uplands High School at Blackridge, inscribed with the words:

1900-1901

DRAWING PRIZE, ADVANCED DIVISION

MADGE TATHAM

The second book was given to her twenty years later. While the high school art prize had been carefully preserved in its embossed leather cover, this book was old and broken, and must have been a favourite: *Mrs Wiggs of the Cabbage Patch*, the sentimental story of a single mother who manages to raise a large family in extreme poverty, through hard work and positive thinking. When Alan Smallie gave it to his wife in 1921, she had five young children, and there was probably a wry comment implicit in the gift. But I would not have paid it any more attention were it not for two words stamped on the frontispiece in a pale italic script.

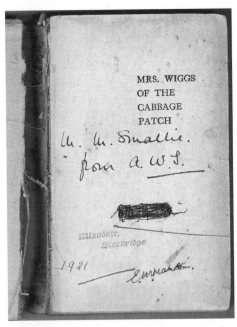

It had been there all the time on the shelf in my mother's room. The name of the house. An address. A trace. Allandale.

I called Francois Marais. No, he said, he wasn't aware of any official record of the name. But as we continued talking, he began to recall having seen it on one of his walks. Yes, he remembered it now, he went on. A gate at Blackridge, with the name Allandale engraved on a white marble post. It would have been Uplands Road, probably number 10.

For the third time, the quest for the Blackridge house seemed to have returned to me after I'd relinquished it.

A bit of research located Faeeza Ballim, who now lived at that address with her husband Mukhtar and their children. I called her and described my mother's garden and the little stream. There had to be water. A stream.

'Oh yes, there's a stream,' she said. 'Or there was. The water isn't flowing any more – people dam it, or divert it higher up.'

As it happened, water was something that Faeeza understood. She was a hydrologist. Glad to talk about her home, she told me how beautiful it was. The big trees. But when I asked about a marble gate and the name Allandale, she knew nothing of it.

'No, there's never been a gate,' she said. 'No signs or anything. But if there's something else we can do, please let us know.'

My next call was to Lyndy Mansfield whose parents, the Smythes, built the house in 1940. She now lived in Durban, but remembered it clearly: a big rambling garden situated below the railway line and above the road, with two streams running through it.

'Oh it was a super childhood at Blackridge,' she said. 'Magical . . . a sort of mystical feel to it.'

She began talking about trees and fruits. Mangoes and bananas and naartjies and Chinese guavas and custard apples. I could hear that she was smiling.

'I don't even know what a custard apple is.'

'If you've ever had one, you'll never forget it. Completely delicious. Oh and mulberries, lots and lots of mulberries. We had absolutely everything.'

It sounded like my mother. Everything. We had absolutely everything.

'For her it was Paradise, you know.'

'Oh yes,' she agreed.

But no, Allandale did not ring a bell.

So I wrote a letter enquiring about the name, and Heiko Bron kindly emailed it to his community network. Did anyone remember it? Nobody did, but Audrey Tanner, the woman who'd left a message on the Gardners'

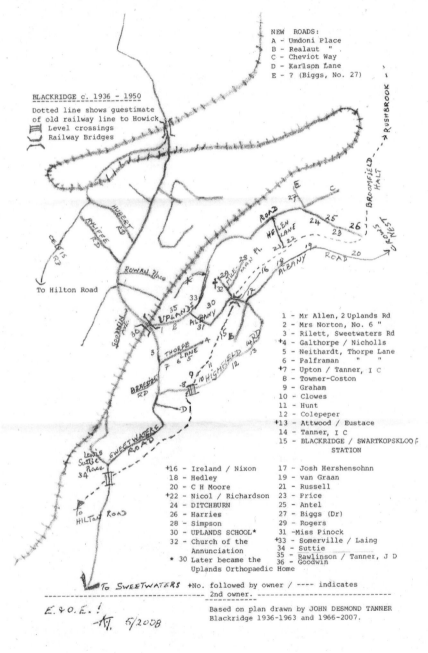

NEW ROADS:
A - Umdoni Place
B - Realaut "
C - Cheviot Way
D - Karlson Lane
E - ? (Biggs, No. 27)

BLACKRIDGE c. 1936 - 1950
Dotted line shows guestimate
of old railway line to Howick
Level crossings
Railway Bridges

To Hilton Road

1 - Mr Allen, 2 Uplands Rd
2 - Mrs Norton, No. 6 "
3 - Rilett, Sweetwaters Rd
+4 - Galthorpe / Nicholls
5 - Neithardt, Thorpe Lane
6 - Palframan " "
+7 - Upton / Tanner, I C
8 - Towner-Coston
9 - Graham
10 - Clowes
11 - Hunt
12 - Colepeper
+13 - Attwood / Eustace
14 - Tanner, I C
15 - BLACKRIDGE / SWARTKOPSKLOOF
      STATION

+16 - Ireland / Nixon
18 - Hedley
20 - C H Moore
+22 - Nicol / Richardson
24 - DITCHBURN
26 - Harries
28 - Simpson
30 - UPLANDS SCHOOL*
32 - Church of the
      Annunciation
* 30 Later became the
      Uplands Orthopaedic Home

17 - Josh Hershensohnn
19 - van Graan
21 - Russell
23 - Price
25 - Antel
27 - Biggs (Dr)
29 - Rogers
31 -Miss Pinock
+33 - Somerville / Laing
34 - Suttie
35 - Rawlinson / Tanner, J D
36 - Goodwin

+No. followed by owner / ---- indicates
2nd owner.

E. & O. E. !
KT. 5/2008

Based on plan drawn by JOHN DESMOND TANNER
Blackridge 1936-1963 and 1966-2007.

answering machine after we visited, sent a map of the area drawn by her husband John who'd lived at Blackridge since 1936.

The lines of the drawing were approximate and personal, but it recorded an intimately attentive memory of the neighbourhood, and I recognised some landmarks. The Church. Uplands School. My mother's railway line. There was no point in looking for the name Smallie because by that date the family had left. And there was no sign of Cyril's family, the Greens, either. But some names did sound familiar. Simpson, Nicholls, Nicol . . .

Suddenly I could hear my mother telling me that their neighbours were the Nicols, and that they lived in a big double-storey house. Out of the myriad conversations at her bedside came the story of the night that David was born.

'I can see him now,' she'd said of her father. 'I can see him jumping over that fence and shouting loudly for Mrs Nicol to come.'

How had I managed to forget this?

I called Lyndy again. Did she remember the Nicol family from her childhood?

'Yes,' she said, 'they lived in a double-storey house. It's still there.'

'I'll just have to go back to Blackridge. Have another look.'

'Well I'd better come with you. That is, if you'd like me to.'

'Of course. Thank you. I'll hire a car and pick you up.'

I wrote a second letter with a picture of my mother's house and posted it to 'The Resident' at all the properties near the Nicols' place in Helen Lane, and Heiko sent out the same enquiry by email. Soon, various Blackridge neighbours began to respond. Dr Silinga called and said she would ask the local councillor if they had any information about the wood-and-iron house in my photograph; Aileen Metherell wrote that the Nicol sisters had lived in the house next door to hers in Helen Lane, though her house was not the one I was looking for; Terry Higginson described his Victorian brick house, which was also a neighbour of the Nicols, and sent me a satellite image on which he had marked all the streams in the area; Jenny Coetzee wrote about the stable that used to be on their property; and Eugene Joubert told me how the old railway servitude had become a sort of wildlife belt, with duiker and bushpig, lots of monkeys, and a healthy population of porcupines. He said there was a family of large grey mongooses at the bottom of his garden, and that there seemed to be a substantial increase in birdlife too, not only in numbers but also in diversity.

The responses were heartwarming. Perhaps the people who lived there now really were a community. And perhaps the railway servitude really had been, as my mother put it, rescued from civilisation. But it was clear that the chance of actually finding the house was very slim. Nobody remembered Allandale, or could place the photograph. The name was gone, the house was gone, and my mother was gone too. Why then did I persist?

An envelope appeared in the post from my cousin Ian Smallie with some family portraits, among them a tiny picture I'd never seen before.

Betty looks about six, and she is holding a stick. Time and the decay of photographic emulsions have rendered the garden so indistinct that it's impossible to make out any detail. But out of the shadowland where she is playing, the body of the child in shorts and a little white shirt gleams bright. Her expression is concentrated and above her head the dark line of the Ridge marks quite precisely the horizon of home.

The image offered no directions, but it spoke of something wordless that I recognised. Her bare feet are muddy from paddling in the stream.

2.

I returned to Pietermaritzburg a couple of weeks later with Lyndy. She was wearing a cerulean jersey and had short grey hair, bright eyes. She'd left home at about the time I was born, but the world changed slowly in those days, and at first our talk was all a child's nostalgia, tracked with smells and food.

Look, there's the swimming pool, we said. The Alexandra Baths. Remember that smell of the chlorine, and the rubber band you had to wear on your ankle? And the bakery, Oxenhams on the corner. Yes, the smell of that bread as you went past, fresh white on a cold morning, nothing like it. And Grey's Hospital, a nasty place. I hurt my knee and it got septic and I had to go in to have it dressed every day. I can still smell it, terrible.

The streets had been renamed for Langalibalele, Chief Albert Luthuli, Peter Kerchoff, Hoosen Haffejee, Alan Paton . . . But the old grid of the colonial city was quite unchanged so that, even as we made our way through the lively traffic of the twenty-first-century African city that our white girls' home town had become, our particular mission that morning invoked irresistibly the routes and landmarks of another place, and we found ourselves travelling along well-worn tracks in the past.[55]

As we headed out of the city centre for Blackridge, the big Friesland cow was still standing outside what was once the Natal Co-operative Dairy. That freshly painted cow was where our milk used to come from, the glass quart bottle with an aluminium cap on the doorstep each morning, a few inches of cream at the top. Next door was the Nestlé factory. What a glorious smell, the chocolate. You would try to keep breathing it in, all the way past.

In Uplands Road, I stopped at the house Lyndy's parents built.

'Oh look,' she said. 'They've cut down the bougainvillea. It used to be like an English rambling garden. Primroses. And violets everywhere. So many violets. It looks all neat now, trimmed.'

Any change is wrong when you return to a beloved childhood home, but the trees were still huge, and Faeeza Ballim greeted us warmly, offering us tea even though she was fasting.

'We're just letting nature take its course,' she said about the jacaranda tree that had fallen across the lawn. 'We wanted to chop it up, but the children play there so much. It's like a huge jungle gym for them.'

I liked her for that, and for the fact that an Indian family could now live at Blackridge, and for the magic crystals she pointed out to us in the rocks.

'My dad found those on our farm at Nottingham Road,' Lyndy explained. 'He set them in the fish pond ... But after a while we filled the pond up. Couldn't handle the noise of the frogs any longer!'

We walked together around the garden, and her stories of fruit and childhood recalled my mother's. She took us to see the custard apple tree, and the Hlambamanzi tree, and the place where the snake bit her when she was picking mealies, and where she used to sit on her horse, no saddle or bridle, reading a book while he ate an apple, and the Chinese guava and the mulberry tree, and where the plum trees used to be, and where the hammock used to hang, and the precise spot where she was married, and the place where the stream always flowed so strongly in summer.

But for all that, the memory of it was her own. This garden had never been my mother's. I knew that immediately.

As we began to leave, Faeeza paused.

'I hope you find ...' her voice trailed off.

'Whatever it is that I'm looking for.'

'Yes. Please let me know.'

I said to Lyndy that I'd like to go back to the abandoned railway line. And then to look around for streams.

With the trains long gone and the pale late-winter veld now growing across the dismantled spine of the Natal Main Line, the place seemed iconic. We stood on the rough grass of the old platform, and I tried to imagine small Betty waiting there on her own for the steam engine to arrive: those first journeys to school that returned in her final years at the nursing home, when she'd find herself once more on a train.

The wrought iron bridge that spanned the grassy railway servitude looked rusty and resilient, like the recollection of a former world that someone had forgotten to remove. But my mother was gone, and the little white house with the dark room at the centre had also disappeared. From the direction of Sweetwaters, a herd of speckled cattle came meandering through, and a tall young man tending them. Perhaps the gift from the dead is the truth of their death. The recognition that the past does not exist (although it also does). That all we have is now.

We left the line and drove around Blackridge in search of water-courses. With no remaining trace of anything called Allandale, and the wood-and-iron house surely demolished, all I had left to locate where my mother once lived were the railway line above, a road below, the horizon of the Ridge in two fading sepia photographs, the fact that it must have been close enough to the Nicols to consider them next-door neighbours, and the presence of a stream running through the garden.

We found the Nicols' double-storey up a little lane using Lyndy's memory and John Tanner's hand-drawn map. It was built of red brick, and for all its size it was nearly hidden by big trees and a tangle of bush. The nearby houses were mostly modern. Face brick, fences, burglar alarms. No sign of a stream.

It had been a dry season. Everyone said so. But after some searching we did find the marks of a watercourse nearby, and a donga that looked as though it must be wet in summer. And some distance away, towards the end of Uplands Road, I noticed a white municipal railing on the side of the road, like the memory of a little bridge. I stopped the car, and got out to look down into a dusty streambed issuing from someone's garden. It was choked with grasses, wild ginger, and bits of garbage. There must still be times of the year when the water flowed, but at the end of winter there was nothing.

Suddenly a fox terrier was licking my hand, jumping up, trembling with eagerness to get into the car. It brought to mind a picture of my

208

grandfather from the Blackridge years. He is smiling and holding a fox terrier in his arms. My grandmother bred big dogs, but this one was his.

Ninety years later, the little animal would not let us go. He wagged and licked and bounded all over me, wriggling and barking with joy.

3.

To enter the Department of Land Affairs where the Deeds Office and the surveyor general's are located, I had to give my name to uniformed guards, pass through a security check, and sign in for the laptop. It was one of those deeply institutional buildings defined by face-brick corridors, grey-green walls, documents on pinboards, and highly polished linoleum floors.

To anyone who does not work in such a place, it looks like an environment in which the logic of numbers and ruled lines governs everything. But Francois was at home there, and everyone we met responded to his gentle smile. After many years' service, he had retired just two days before. Now he was back for the morning to help me search for the property.

'Oh Mr Marais!' a young woman said, smiling. 'Can't you get enough of us?'

While I watched, he began a meticulous process of tracking, starting with the erf numbers of portions of land from a survey map and filling two pages of my notebook with notes and figures. Each step he explained to me carefully, but it was difficult to follow him through the maze of lines and numbers, properties and portions.

This is it, I thought. Truly the end of the search. If we did not manage to track down Allandale that morning in the Deeds Office, I would finally accept that it was not to be found, that the journey itself had been the destination.

The key element was the stream. Two years before, Francois had sent me survey maps of the area around a stream near Thorpe Lane. This time we were looking for a watercourse near the Nicols' house. After more than an hour he narrowed the search to Erf 526, 'bounded on the

North by Townlands and a stream'. It was surveyed in 1886 during the first critical period of development after the railway reached Pietermaritzburg.

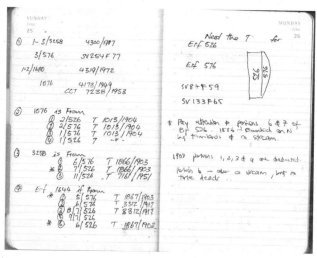

We took the lift to another room to search for the records of its ownership. The Land Register was stored on an ancient microfiche, and it took a while of tracking back and forth, but finally Francois found it. The document showed that the stream flowed through two properties owned by Mr Ireland (Outfitter) which were subsequently transferred to Mr Davie, and then in 1922 to Rosa Helen Nicoll.[56] Okay. So this would have been where the double-storey house stood in what is now called Helen Lane. It was very close, but it was not my mother's stream. Francois looked tired and sorry.

'Do you think we could just try one more thing?' I asked. 'That other streambed I saw near the end of Uplands Road?'

It's not easy to find a tiny watercourse among the survey diagrams of a whole neighbourhood. But I felt we simply could not leave the Deeds Office without a look at the place with the white municipal railing where Lyndy and I had met the fox terrier.

So Francois patiently began the whole process again, tracking dates and numbers. After an extensive search, he concluded that the portion I was seeking had been misfiled, and went downstairs to look again on the computer.

It was while I was waiting for him that the absurdity of my quest really came home to me. What strange determination had enlisted his help and that of so many other generous people, and brought me all the way from Cape Town to this neon-lit room in a bleak Government building to look for ... What? What really was I looking for? And why?

The room was quiet. In the quietness, I imagined I could sense for a moment the mass of pain and power encoded in the documents which were housed in the building.

This is the place, I realised. This is the place where the records of conquest and dispossession are all kept safe, where every tract of land is mapped, numbered, filed, and scrupulously catalogued. This is the very place where the brutal occupation of the living world is secured.

Once you've built a railway line, it's easier to take possession. Things and people may be transported swiftly up and down its spine. Roads and so-called properties appear quite naturally along its flanks. The lively, various world becomes a map, and the cartographic view that sees all from above becomes the way things are. By the mid-1880s when the neighbourhood of Blackridge had begun to take shape on either side of the new line, erf numbers and title deeds conferred quite literally on those who acquired them a sense of entitlement. And in the broader environment of the Colony, things seemed to be looking good for the settlers and their wars.

As I waited that morning beside the aged microfiche machine in a building stacked with the documents of ownership, for just a moment I glimpsed the strange collective complicity by which we continue to believe in them. How many humans and other beings had died for these imagined lines?[57] For a moment, I felt the sadness of it. The deluded, mindless, greedy madness of it. My ancestors and their wars. The particular war we now inherit. This war against the earth, the watercourses, the forests, the grasslands, and against all beings, human and non-human. Our war.

Francois returned carrying two more microfiche tapes of Land Register records. It still felt extraordinary that at the heart of the state repository was a man – now just retired, but returned for a few hours – who had hundreds of erf numbers in his head, who understood its workings better than anyone else, and whose favourite thing was walking in the wild. My guide through the labyrinth.

He smiled gently. 'Let's see what we have here.'

Scanning through the first microfiche in the archaic machine, he clicked and whirred through a mass of documents. There was nothing relevant. We were looking for records relating to the ownership of Lot 512 PMB, a plot towards the end of Uplands Road that appeared from the survey map as though it might just have a stream in it.

He inserted the second tape, and we began to check through.

All of a sudden, I grabbed his knee. 'There it is!'

On the shadowy blue speckled screen of the microfiche was a hand-written list of property transactions. Among them was my grandfather's name, Alan W Smallie.

Afterwards, Francois said, 'I'll never forget that moment of excitement.'

It was a glimpse of something incongruously intimate. Family. I shouted out the name.

The transfer documents and the original survey diagram were stored in a great old file of ageing papers. It was all both ordinary and completely unexpected. I read everything in a state of astonishment.

Lot 512 PMB was surveyed by the town surveyor, a man called George Holgate, in August 1884. It was precisely that triumphalist moment when the British had recently won the Zulu War, the Natal Government Railways line was making its way north, and Frances Stocker was writing her novel on the Mooi River farm.

The survey diagram was confidently drawn, and there was something tender and meticulous about Holgate's work. I savoured the fine inked lines of his directional arrows, the beautiful lettering, the careful colouring-in of red Railway, brown Road, blue Watercourse, and the green shading of the land. During its passage through generations of files, the document had become a palimpsest of successive scripts, but the original drawing identified exactly the defining features that my mother had always described: the railway above, the road below, and a stream running through the garden.

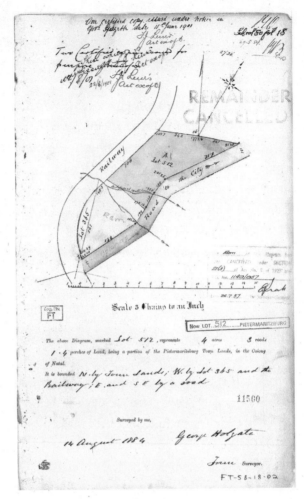

The precise moment of history and ownership that Holgate's drawing records felt significant, but in a way that I could only articulate as a question: what is it that happens on that first particular day when a place becomes a property, and a little seasonal stream (a world with frogs in it and dragonflies skimming the surface, and maybe some weaver birds building nests) becomes a narrow blue line to be filed on a shelf in a government building with polished linoleum floors and men in dark uniforms guarding the entrance?

The trace of his living hand on the creamy paper had personalised the drawing of Lot 512 and made it poignant in a way that the current survey diagrams of the neighbourhood could never be. Yet still it was a map, an imaginary view composed of measurements, ruled lines, and partitions, constructed for the sole purpose of taking possession.

The first man who arrived to occupy the site in 1884 was called Daniel Faber Whittaker. Others came after him, but the deed of transfer that interested me was a piece of paper which records that, on the ninth day of the month of August in the year of Our Lord One Thousand Nine Hundred and Nineteen, the land was truly and legally sold to my grandfather for five hundred and seventy-five pounds sterling. It is noted that he had a mortgage, and that the details of rates and drainage were all in order. The information was sparse and bureaucratic, but somehow it was enough.

Later that afternoon a message from Michael appeared on Google Chat.
Hey.
Hello.
Have you found *it*?
Yes.
Wow.
We found the title deeds. The place was sold by James Lawson (Tailor) to Alan Watson Smallie (Schoolmaster) in 1919.
Schoolmaster??
He had a job at the Tech.
OK.
A certain piece of freehold land, in extent four acres, three roods and one decimal four perches. Lot 512 of the Town Lands of the City of Pietermaritzburg, Province of Natal. A stream, a horse, cows, orchards, vegetables, trees of every kind . . .
Paradise.
Yes absolutely.

When Alan Smallie bought the property, the Great War was over. He had given up working for profiteering bosses, and his new job at the Technical College meant he could afford a mortgage. The season was late winter, and the date of transfer was a few days after my mother's first birthday. It would have been at Blackridge that she learnt how to walk.

215

4.

Dusk comes early in Pietermaritzburg. By the time I drove back to Uplands Road, the light was already beginning to fade.

'It's a homesick time,' my mother used to say when I told her as a child about the inexplicable sadness I always felt at dusk. On this particular day, the sadness made a kind of good sense. In the changing light, you can experience how things change.

I stopped the car beside the fox terrier's dry streambed and used a contemporary survey map to count off the five current properties into which the original plot had been divided. Four acres is a big garden by any standard. To Betty and Cyril, it was the whole world.

Starting at the first property with the lemon trees at the far end of Uplands Road, I walked along the length of the fence, looking in. The land sloped upwards towards the railway line, and it was planted with trees and shrubs and lawns, poinsettias and azaleas, a big tree heavy with bright naartjies, a house on each plot, and no sign at all of wood-and-iron. From the other side of the fence, fierce dogs barked at me, and the friendly fox terrier had disappeared.

This was it. I had found what I was looking for. Too shy or bewildered to ring a doorbell and cross the threshold, I simply walked along the boundary, peering in.

And then at the final garden I came to a place that felt like the beginning. The house was obscured by a great hedge, huge wild trees, and rambling creepers. An old treehouse was perched among high branches. A long driveway, hedged on either side with ferns and deep azaleas, disappeared up the slope into the green.

For a long time, I stood at the gate. My mother's home.

I would find out who lived there, and visit the following day. Whoever it was, I knew I could trust them. In the late light the pink azalea petals against the dark foliage gleamed like beacons.

By some curious magic, the next day was 3 August. It would have been her ninety-fourth birthday, and almost exactly ninety-three years since the transfer of the property.

As I drove through the gate, a pale Labrador and a young fox terrier came down the azalea driveway to meet me, smiling and wagging their tails. I'd spoken to Natalie Blackmore the previous evening, and when I told her my story, she'd been friendly and seemed delighted.

'Of course,' she said. 'As long as you don't mind that the house is in chaos. My mother-in-law died last year and we're sorting through her stuff.'

'You know Natalie, I just knew I could trust people with a garden like that.'

'You mean messy?'

'No. Just abundant, wild, beautiful. All those azaleas.'

Now she was waiting for me at the end of the driveway, a dark-haired, dark-eyed woman with a warm smile. The house behind her was substantial and generously proportioned, with bay windows and a large verandah, probably built in the late 1920s, just after the Smallies sold the place and before the Depression made builders economise on quality.

'Let me show you the garden first,' she said, 'and then we can have some tea.'

She described how she and her husband Andrew had looked at fifty-eight houses before finding this one. They'd made a list of all the features it had to have, and others that would be a bonus. It had everything.

'Like?'

'Well, various things. But trees especially. It had to have trees. This feeling of being isolated in nature.'

She showed me the big avocado trees, the naartjies, the very old lemon trees, the tangled palms, and the enormous pecan tree that was brought down in a great storm. Once you were in the garden, the strongest impression was of being surrounded by trees and high creepers, and the dense green of many kinds of foliage. The dogs followed us everywhere.

'And is there still a mango tree?'

'No, not in our garden.'

For a moment, I felt a sense of regret. But after all, what did it matter? The actual trees might have been supplanted by others, yet I recognised them anyway. These really were my mother's trees. A hundred colours, all called green.

And then I noticed the stand of bamboo at the back of the garden. It was tatty and unromantic, an impenetrable hedge of fine canes overgrown with black-eyed Susan and tangled with blade wire along the boundary to the railway servitude. The bamboo was growing in that unvisited part of a large property where planks are left to rot and pipes to rust, and an old ceramic sink fills up with dry leaves and the homes of insects. As any gardener will tell you, once you've planted bamboo it's almost ineradicable. A single plant sends out rhizomes underground that come up as new shoots some distance away, and they spread and spread, become a dense grove.

The sight of it dislodged a childhood memory of my mother telling me about having to go past the bamboo to get to the outhouse. At night, when the wind made strange noises in the canes and the darkness was full of bats, her brother Barts would walk with her when she needed the lavatory. He didn't really mind, she said. He understood she was frightened. Later, at school in Pietermaritzburg, she had to find her way all alone. It was her first day and the thing had a metal flush chain she'd never seen before. She pulled the chain, and it made such a terrible noise that she knew she must have broken it. For years she told nobody, but the horror of breaking the lavatory on that first day at school remained with her for the rest of her life.

'Let's have tea,' Natalie said. 'Then you can explore some more. As long as you like.'

The wild proliferation of things in the house was like another region of the garden. A mass of blue glass bottles caught the sunlight in a window. Hundreds of wooden spoons hung on the kitchen wall. There were multitudes of books on shelves and tables. And all the orchids from her huge collection in the greenhouse that were currently in flower had been brought inside the house. At the dining room table a woman was holding up a magnifying glass to a faded sepia photograph. Heaped around her were more photographs, ageing handwritten documents, a silver hairbrush, pieces of porcelain. Natalie introduced her sister-in-law, Susan.

'Sorry about all this,' she said. 'I'm here on a visit to work through my mother's things. Researching her life. She died last year.'

'I understand. That's just what I'm doing.'

The three of us had tea together in the kitchen, several rounds. We talked about the house and the garden, about mothers and daughters, about the excavation of the past, and the affinity one senses with particular places, and we wondered what it is about the wildness of rambling gardens that makes some people feel at home. Natalie was a marine biologist, and Susan taught English in Portugal though she'd been trained as an archaeologist. At first, she was quiet, but gradually she began to talk.

'We like to have a material thing from the past, don't we? Whether it is a ruin, or an object like a silver hairbrush, or a letter . . .'

'Yes exactly.'

'But really, you know,' she continued, 'this is a spiritual journey.'

219

Somehow the intimacy of her particular quest had opened the door to an answering intimacy with mine. Sitting together drinking tea in the kitchen, generations of social reserve melted away or became irrelevant. My grandmother would have taken tea with the Blackridge ladies not far from where we were sitting, while her daughters served sandwiches, cake, and biscuits, and her husband hid out in his workshop. But this meeting in the kitchen was quite simple and direct. It felt like innocence, like Betty and Cyril playing barefoot in the garden.

I showed them my few photographs.

'I think that's an avo tree,' Natalie said, using her magnifying class to look at the tiny image of Betty sitting on a cane chair, with Bindle at her feet. 'But let's see if we can work out where the house would have been.'

We walked around the garden holding up the little pictures against the horizon to match the Ridge in the photographs to the bare line of the hill, and passing Susan's magnifying glass between us like three Fates. Natalie had the keenest eyes and a penetrating determination to understand what she was seeing.

'There's the bamboo hedge!' she said at last, pointing to the background of the picture of Betty with her dolls.

'You're right! And that corrugated iron structure nearby must have been the outhouse.'

At once the image had a location in the world. I watched as Natalie continued to scrutinise it and the other photographs closely, looking not at the people and the house in the foreground as I had always done, but at the structure of the environment in which they were situated: a low wall, a wooden trellis, a stone path, a levelled area of ground, the angle of the hill behind the house, the orientation of light.

We searched then for traces in the actual garden, in the area east of the bamboo. It was like looking for bones or broken artefacts, the half-buried skeleton of a place. The dogs sniffed and followed. After a while I found the remains of a mossy brick path, buried in bamboo leaves, that led towards the neighbouring garden.

'I think that's where it was,' Natalie said, pointing. 'The house.'

It was overgrown and tangled on the other side of the fence, but we could see a level piece of ground, some crumbling steps, and what looked like paths to nowhere. My mother's house.

Natalie and Susan left me then to sit or meander on my own. The azaleas were in full flower, and the old roses had tight pink buds just beginning to open. The garden was deep in maidenhairs and bracken, masses of wild ginger and delicious monsters, walls entirely covered with tickey creeper. And all the trees. I sat on the lawn for a long time, playing with the young fox terrier. The day was full of birds.

As I was leaving, with an invitation to return and meet the family, Natalie said, 'What do you think it is? How do people come to love particular places, to appreciate them, to sense the quality of a place, to understand what they *are*? Do you think it's learnt, or something that you just either have or don't have?'

'I don't know. Maybe learnt.'

But then, who's the teacher? For my mother, it seems to have been the place itself.

5.

That afternoon I met Andrew, the librarian who'd helped me at the very beginning of my search and had to give up looking for the house because he became ill. At exactly three thirty he was waiting at the Botanical Garden's tea house, a tall, good-looking young man with a shy smile.

It had seemed like an evocative place to meet. Like the other national botanical gardens around the Empire, it was set up to be a vital node in a global network. Soon after its establishment in 1874, the garden became a key site for the cultivation of useful and ornamental plants, and a base for their distribution across the Colony. Exotic trees, fruits, and flowers, tracked through this point from everywhere to everywhere: wattle and eucalyptus in particular, and azaleas too, which grew well and were said to be especially popular. A century later, it was a location in my own childhood, but Andrew had never been there before. After all, what place would there have been for an Indian boy at Bot Gardens in those years, while I was feeding the ducks or having crumpets with my mother?

We ordered cheesecake to celebrate her birthday, and I told him how I'd finally discovered the plot of land he'd helped to track down. He was happy that the story had an ending.

'And now I've found another bit of it for you,' he said. 'Just a trace.'

It was Andrew who first pointed me in the direction of Alan Smallie's military career. Now he told me about someone called Parbhoo Singh who'd been there too.

Parbhoo was an indentured labourer on the same site of human exploitation and carbon extraction that made my Tatham great-grandfather rich, the Dundee Coal Mine. But during the Siege of Ladysmith, he was given a new job: to climb up a certain tree and wave a flag to

warn the British troops whenever he saw a flash from one of the Boers'
Long Toms on Mbulwana. There were twenty-two seconds between the
instant of the cannon's flash and the moment when the shell burst into
the town. So his role was critical. After the War, at a special ceremo-
ny in the Durban City Hall, the Viceroy of India presented him with a
Kashmir robe in recognition of the brave task he had carried out.[58]

'It struck a chord in me,' Andrew said.

'Indeed.'

'I suppose some people would have said he was a good coolie.'

'At least he had a name.'

I told him about the lullaby of the cannon on Mbulwana during the
Siege, and about my grandfather writing down the words '*Ja sahib, kona
pudding*'. He spoke about his own ancestors. Yes, they too had been
indentured workers come out from India, but he knew very little about
them. He'd grown up in Northdale, a designated Indian area under the
Group Areas Act, and he now lived in Lincoln Meade.

'It's a so-called cosmopolitan neighbourhood, you know. Sometimes
I find I don't know what my neighbours expect of me.'

After tea, we walked through the tall avenue of London plane trees
planted in 1908, two years after the Bhambatha Rebellion. Our feet
scuffed up piles of dry leaves, just as they did when I was a child, and I
spoke about the pieces of pottery from the Botanical Garden site that
I'd seen in the museum storeroom. The big pots glued together from
broken fragments. Gavin Whitelaw's meticulous drawings. The boxes of
ceramic shards from the closest sites to Blackridge.

'You know how it is,' I said. 'I wanted to imagine who was here before.
The colonial narrative takes up so much space. It's just so loud.'

Generations before the recent history that entangled Andrew's ancestors with mine, someone lived with friends and family in the lush green
place that became Bot Garden, and left behind an earthenware vessel
near the river. That vessel is now irretrievably smashed, but in the excavated fragments you can still touch the pattern: marks of a living body,
trace of a fingernail in the wet clay.

6.

The dogs barked fiercely when I reached the gate of the house next door to Natalie's. There were two Rottweilers and a fox terrier. I'm always wary around big dogs, but then a man appeared from the house, wearing jeans and a T-shirt. His face was sensitive and he had a greying moustache. He greeted me and smiled. We all relaxed.

Sitting in Ian de Villiers' sitting room, I told him my story. He was a qualified diesel mechanic and a biker, and he talked about living alone with his teenage children, and about his father who was eighty-four.

'He's coming here soon,' he said. 'My sister and I sort of share him. Trying to keep him out of a care home. He's been lost since my mother died.'

Then Ian took me up to the back of the garden, the overgrown place I'd seen from Natalie's side of the fence. He said he understood what I was doing, that whenever he went back to Beaufort West he would look for his grandfather's house.

'I haven't found it yet.'

'So you do understand?'

'Oh yes, absolutely.'

The modern house was at the front of his plot, probably built in the sixties. Behind it the whole design of the garden, a pattern of old stone paths and terraces, led up the slope through avocado trees and azaleas and wild ginger to an unkempt place at the back where the land had once been levelled and a low wall outlined the edge of another terrace. Ian held up my photographs against the horizon, and matched the line of the Ridge precisely.

'But I'm trying to make sense of exactly where the house was,' he said, pacing out the space.

Once again someone I'd never met before was doing whatever they could to help me. He seemed apologetic about the wildness of the garden.

'I just can't bear cutting trees.'

'Please don't worry. It's beautiful.'

Then he showed me the course of Betty and Cyril's stream, how in summer it runs down from the Ridge through his land and into Phindile Shange's property next door. Ian's daughter, Michelle, used to play in the water with the neighbour's children, and he once found a freshwater crab in a bucket in her bedroom. That night, when she was sleeping, he released it back into the stream.

'Stay as long as you like,' he said, leaving me to be on my own. 'And when it's time to go and see Phindile, just walk through the gate in the fence. It was made for the children when they were young.'

What happens if some day you reach your destination?

My mother's house is a low garden wall with ferns in the cracks. Her moss is green and the colour of rust. My mother's house is a lemon tree laden with yellow fruit. There are moles underground. Creepers twine and spiral. Hydrangeas in the terraced beds have gone to seed. The bamboo grows high along the back fence, sheds paper leaves on the paths, makes noises in the wind at night. The fox terrier follows me everywhere, chases the drifting fairy seeds of the kapok tree as they puff from the pod and fly. My mother's house is a well in the ground, and the glossy leaves that grow out of it. There are primulas and dense clover at my feet, and her deep lichen grows on all the trees. Her house is a stonemason's spiral form and four steps leading to a stand of wild ginger, the flowers clear orange against the green. Her house is a maze of paths to nowhere built on diagonal lines that I cannot interpret, stone slabs covered with moss and dandelions, hidden under dry leaves. My mother's house is a levelled plain occupied by grass. It is a derelict maid's quarters. It is layer on layer of human habitation, all the way back. It is the quiet of forgotten things and unwalked paths. Snowdrops are blooming in my mother's house. The day is full of birds and insects. The sky is clear.

A teenage girl came towards me up the path from Ian's place. Pale slender face, long dark hair, cellphone, a sensitive smile. Michelle.

'You really are so lucky to have grown up here,' I said.

'Oh I know. I love it.'

Then she showed me the mulberry tree where she and her friend used to build forts, and the place where they would camp out at night, and the stream where the crabs live. She said she had told her dad that if robbers ever came she would always know where to hide. She knew *all* the places.

'When my mother lived here,' I told her, 'she and her friend used to hide up in the big mango tree, or under the house. And they played in the stream, like you. It was all one big property then. They had cows, chickens . . . Even a horse.'

'Oh and now there are all those fences!'

She looked troubled, but then her face cleared. 'I would so love to live on a farm. Just that size. There was a horse here once, you know. Just for a few days. I rescued it.'

Then she showed me the way through the children's gate to the other side of the fence. I walked through the gate, and introduced myself to the owner, Phindile Shange.

Her garden was more open than Ian's or Natalie's, a spacious lawn surrounded by trees. There used to be more trees, she said, but one night she came home and there were two men hiding in the bushes.

'I hate cutting down trees. But this time I had to do it. You know how it is. Crime. In summer the stream runs right through the lawn.'

We sat together on the grass, and she told me how she'd fallen in love with the place when she first saw it, and how her children had grown up in the garden. Zimisele and Lwazi, and her niece Sbulelo. Now they were older and not really interested, but her extended family brought their little ones to play, and the stream was a magnet for the neighbourhood children. Some of them still came for sleepovers.

'When you're a child you really enjoy this sort of place,' she said. 'I love hearing their happy voices when they're playing. It's beautiful. I think everyone in Blackridge knows this stream.'

Phindile had gentle dark eyes and a generous smile. Her work was in the Provincial Legislature, but it was Saturday and she had been cooking when I arrived. Sitting together on the grass, our words flowed like a river, and it seemed just perfect that it was she who was the guardian of the stream.

We talked about our children, and she told me about hers who are now grown and thoroughly globalised.

'They don't really think about race at all,' she said. 'But yes, it's all going to take a long time.'

I told her about my mother making mud pies from the stream, and about our lullaby and Joseph Shabalala's translation.

She asked me to sing it, and when I did, she nodded.

'I wouldn't have been sure of the vocab. But yes, I know it. *Ehe* . . .'

I laughed.

'I wonder when I last heard someone say "*ehe*". Living in the Cape I miss hearing isiZulu spoken.'

We talked about home and about home food. Phindile spoke about *uputhu*, and how these days your children grow up to have different tastes.

'For me, *uphuthu* is soul food,' I said. 'The woman who looked after me when I was a child used to make it. Her name was Eslina. I've often tried, but I never seem to get it right.'

'Oh you should have told me! I would have made you *uphuthu*.'

Then she carefully explained how to cook it properly, the real way.

When we said goodbye, she promised to send pictures of the stream in summer.

At the far end of the original plot was Kelsey's garden. She showed me tracks and traces, and picked up things other people had left behind. She knew all the paths.

Kelsey was nine. She had steady dark eyes and apple cheeks, soft baby skin, and a pair of blue boots decorated with red hearts and flowers. She lived with her parents and two Alsatians.

'We think it may once have been an avo farm,' her mother Cairie Bartman said. 'There are so many trees. Though the people before us did cut down quite a few. They had a sick child, and I think it was all too much for them. They also painted the walls purple.'

'So you had to see beyond all that.'

'Yes. For me, cutting down trees is terrible.'

It was what I kept hearing.

'I've been planting more,' she went on. 'And roses.'

'And is there still a mango tree?'

I told her about Betty and Cyril's hiding place.

'No, not any more. But you know I grew up in Zimbabwe with a mango tree and we used to sit up in the branches and eat them all day.'

Kelsey led me around her garden, pointing things out, unearthing shards and traces. An ancient plough with a climbing rose beginning to cover it. An old iron stake poking out from the ground. A hollow tree where the mongooses used to live. A massive rusty screw from the railway days. Last vestiges of the Iron Age, Victorian.

'And look over here,' she said. 'The paths go under the fence.'

It was a wide old path built of stone and brick that exactly matched the ones in Ian's garden. The path was mossy, obscured by leaves, and it ran straight through from one plot to the next, a path ignorant of fences or Vibracrete walls or the current lines of ownership. What do you do with such a path?

Kelsey and I sat on the broken steps of the old path with the Alsatians beside us and talked about digging things up from the past.

Inside the house she showed me the lucky horseshoe on her bedroom door. She had found it in the garden when her mother was planting the rose bed. I told her the story of Shandy, my grandfather's horse who had three times survived becoming horsemeat during the Siege of Lady-smith, and ended his days in the garden at Blackridge.

'So I think we can say that was Shandy's horseshoe, don't you?'

Kelsey smiled.

'Cool!'

When at last I said I needed to go, she held out two artefacts: the huge rusty screw and the remains of a heavy implement with a sharp point like the beak of some predatory bird. Her small hands holding the heavy tools were soft and dimpled, the pink skin smooth as roses.

'No really, Kelsey. They're yours.'

But she was sure and quite insistent.

'For you. Take them.'

That evening at the Blackmores' house I met Katie, Natalie's daughter. She was fifteen, a tall young woman with long curly hair and a laughing smile. For her the garden had been a magic place, another world in the midst of this one.

'She really was a fairy child,' her mother said quietly. 'I used to have to know where all the fairy gardens were, so that I could come and take a little bite. Leave some tiny thing.'

Katie was a student at Epworth, my old school where my mother and Mary Gardner were both teachers. We talked about the Blackridge garden, and about school and common friends. It was a long time since she'd put out tea parties for the fairies, but she showed me her bedroom which was still hung with stars, and in her cupboard was a belly-dancing skirt made of green satin and stitched with sequins, a heap of glass bracelets, a silver shimmering veil, and a hoop entwined with silk flowers.

Her father Andy, an environmental lawyer, seemed almost opposite. Yet a sort of methodical curiosity, derived perhaps from his training, enabled him to perform a different kind of magic on my mother's photographs.

Like everyone else I'd met, he brought his own particular quality of attention to my eccentric quest. So instead of simply scrutinising the picture of the wood-and-iron house, he used his high-quality tech to scan it, and project the image onto the wall. Suddenly two figures I'd never noticed before appeared on the verandah. A young man at the top of the stairs, and a young woman facing him at the threshold. Andy continued to look closely.

'Is that Betty?' he said. And then, 'No it can't be. Too grown up. Probably an older sister. Let's look at the ones of her and Cyril.'

There was a curious intimacy in hearing their names spoken.

'Look at her dress,' he said. 'That ribbon in her hair . . . Or is it a ribbon?'

Just then, Andy's sister Susan walked in and saw the two best friends standing in the room before us, life-size.

'Oh look at them from here!' she said. 'It makes me quite emotional.'

The children's faces, bodies, hands, and bare feet were more distinct than I'd ever seen them. They were standing together in the living room in the very place that used to be the garden. They were smiling.

7.

'There's something about a wood-and-iron house,' Graham Tegg said, when I visited him the next day. 'It's home. It's *really* home.'

He was a tall man in a baseball cap, long shorts, and sandals. His place was not far from the old railway station, and it adjoined the patch of forest I'd photographed for my mother, the picture she'd asked me to stick across her TV screen. The house itself, nearly hidden from the road by high trees, was what hers might have been like were it still standing. But the state of dereliction in which I found it could not have been further removed from the polished floors and scrubbed walls of the home my grandmother kept.

Graham seemed to take a particular interest in the marks of impermanence. He showed me the wooden front step that had been worn down by people's feet, the brown shadow on the white door from the dogs, and the old bath now rusting in the grass beside a broken stove, its enamel thinned by years of naked bodies.

'Time goes on,' he said.

Outside, the corrugated iron walls had once been painted pale green. Inside, the rooms were wood-panelled, white tongue-and-groove, the corners neatly joined, the house filled up with furniture from another era. He explained that there was a time when you could order the whole kit from England. They shipped it out and assembled it on site.

'Your mother's house would have been one of those. But wood-and-iron is not really suited to this climate. The Mistbelt. It's just too damp.'

We sat on the verandah drinking Oros, with two old Alsatians at our knees. Graham pointed out the rag stuffed into a window-pane.

'I just can't find a replacement for the old glass. Just look at the new stuff on the other window. It's chalk and cheese.'

Though he made some low-level apologies about needing to get around to fixing things up, I had the sense that he was really not worried by the state of the place. Or rather, it seemed that, after the stroke, his energy was reduced and his mind no longer worked like other people's. It was not interested in being soaped down or neatened up. It wanted to be outside. And it was not much concerned that the car and the motorbike and the roof were rusting away, or that the avos were dropping to the ground for the dogs to eat, or that an abundance of oranges and lemons ripened on the trees and fell.

'Nice for people who can use them,' he said about the fruit.

And then, 'Everything has a story.'

He pointed to the seemingly random collection of things assembled on shelves on the verandah. There were enamel mixing bowls, pieces of old iron, a pile of bonsai pots, a wooden box stamped with the name of Crerar's Cool Drinks, a great ball of twine . . .

'You just have to look at it closely?'

'Yes. That's my mother's cake tin. These are stones from the Kimberley diamond diggings before they started the Big Hole.'

As we walked around Graham's plot, I came to understand that his place was not so much a cultivated home-and-garden as a temporary clearing in the Mistbelt forest that he took care to nurture and observe. The trees were fabulous, the tallest I'd seen in Blackridge. Two high Victorian palms stood at the entrance. Massive cabbage trees and several other great ones that looked hundreds of years old grew into the sky. And there were groves of wild bananas.

He told me about the four thousand clivias he'd planted.

'They're very dear to my heart, you know. Clivias. Unfortunately they're also dear to the taste buds of the moles. The dogs hunted the moles, so the clivias had to go.'

When he spoke about animals and plants, he was clearly talking about his friends. I told him about my mother, the decay of her memory, and the picture of the piece of forest across her TV.

'You know,' he said, 'I used to have to go in there and take the traps apart. Lasso-type traps set with cabbage for the monkeys. People shoot them and trap them. But we're in *their* territory, as far as I'm concerned.'

A hawk flew overhead.

'The hawks eat the babies: hadeda chicks and monkeys.'

Graham paused, and then added, 'Oh well, it's just part of the pattern of it all.'

It could have been my mother speaking.

He went on, 'A friend of mine came here and counted twenty-seven species of birds.'

Together we wandered along stone paths and steps that looked as though they'd been built by the same hands that made the hundred-year-old paths through Ian's and Kelsey's gardens at the far end of Uplands Road. Broken, resilient, moss-covered, scattered with leaves . . . on the old paths, the tread of forgotten feet was both remembered and obliterated.

Then Graham took me to the place where he used to sit outside every night in the pitch pitch black before the massive fig tree fell.

'I'd sit there for an hour, an hour and a half,' he said. 'The bats come right in, you know. Beautiful. Sometimes you see an owl. Then one night there was this light in the forest. I went over to see, and there were guys with catapults, shooting hadedas. I couldn't believe it. It made my stomach turn.'

'How horrible.'

I asked about the fig tree, and he told me how one branch after another had just come down.

'It was clear days. No wind, nothing. All I can think is that . . . he committed suicide. The tree just committed suicide.'

Once the tree had fallen, Graham's shelter from the rest of the world was ruptured. Before that the wood-and-iron house was invisible.

'It used to be dark here,' he told me. 'Deep shade. You couldn't see in. Now the last of the clivias are getting sunburnt.'

'Do you think it will grow back?' I asked. 'It looks like it's trying to send out new shoots.'

'Yes,' he said, and his voice sounded tired. 'He's trying.'

8.

'It's not just that something's been lost. It's that it's been broken. Smashed.'

John Wright's words kept returning to me. And at the same time, my mother's voice saying, 'I feel like an egg that's been smashed.'

Now, six months after her death, I had found the house and knew with certainty that it too had been destroyed. But it was Sunday morning, and Francois was waiting for me outside St Mary's. He was dressed not for church but for a hike to the top of the Ridge.

'Just smell that jasmine,' he said.

Masses of white jasmine had run wild up the trees, and I picked a sprig to carry with us: the scent of her birthday at Blackridge, early August. At the vanished railway station, a rusting iron stake still bore the words 'GLASGOW LONDON', but the only trace left of the platform was a low brick wall alive with ferns. Beyond that, the wild banana groves were full of birds, the aloes were in flower, and a herd of morning cattle from the other side of the Ridge were grazing where the line used to run.

We crossed the abandoned railway servitude and took a wide dirt road up the Ridge through the eucalyptus plantation. When I'd visited before with the family, these particular trees had just been planted. Now they were growing tall and straight on either side. Regiments in rows. Thousands upon thousands. Clones.

Higher up, the road continued to climb, but as we reached the summit of the hill, the plantation on the right side of the track gave way to golden veld grass. On our previous visit to Blackridge, I thought my mother's grassland had all been eradicated and replaced by monoculture. But once again, I was simply not seeing what was there. High on the hill, the veld was still alive. Wild.

Francois explained that the road we were now walking along the spine of the Ridge marked the dividing line between what was called 'Pieter-maritzburg Town and Townlands' and the King's Land.

'The King?'

'King Goodwill Zwelithini. It's owned by the Ingonyama Trust and the king is the trustee, so it's referred to as the King's Land.'

'And when was that division made?'

'1850.'

'So the British annexed Natal in 1844, and already by 1850 they were carving it up. I guess by then they'd started shipping in settlers.'

'Yes. It was Grant 1637, I think, that set aside the land for PMB Town and Townlands.'

Once again Francois showed that rare ability to combine a love of walking and the outdoors with the meticulous precision of the surveyor general's records.

'I think the grant to the native reserve was later,' he continued. 'Grant 4669, if I remember correctly. The grant numbers were registered in the Deeds Office according to a page number, so this was early.'

As we walked, he talked about Theophilus Shepstone who was appointed Diplomatic Agent to the Native Tribes in 1846, and went on to become the highly influential Secretary for Native Affairs. Walking steadily uphill, he explained how Shepstone's policies created the so-called native reserves in the Colony of Natal and determined people's access to land. At first, Francois said, he seemed to get on well with African people, to 'understand' them, as they say. But this fairly soon changed, and by 1878 he was supporting Sir Bartle Frere and Lord Chelmsford in their determination to go to war with the amaZulu.

'So they found some silly pretext and delivered an ultimatum to Cetshwayo.'

'Such a disaster. So terribly divisive.'

'Yes,' he said. 'The whole history of the region could have been different.'

The sky was blue, the day warm. The road we were walking ran the length of the Ridge, a deep scar that split the land in two. On our left, the plantation. On our right, the veld. Beyond on either side, the world of plants and people and other beings was marked with the consequences of that first dividing line.

We stopped at the summit near the beacon stone at the edge of the old native reserve, the place where the lines of occupation cross.

Voortrekkers came this way in their wagons, but their tenure was brief. By the late 1840s, with Natal under British rule, thousands of English-speaking immigrants had begun to appear, many of them driven from their native land by poverty or semi-poverty, bringing with them the promise of trade and civilisation and respectability, and the right to claim farms, build houses, schools, and churches, raise cattle and sheep, plant maize and wattle and sugar and beautiful gardens, and to compete with the local black inhabitants for space in the newly emerging colonial order. Within thirty years, their presence had provoked a bloody civil war.[59]

From where we were sitting on Whale Back, as Francois called the Ridge, you could see the whole region.

The uncultivated veld on our right led down to a dense belt of indigenous bush growing on the Vulindlela side of the slope. It looked diverse and lively, inhabited by birds and very old trees: the characteristic Mistbelt 'mosaic' ecosystem of grassland and forest. Below the ancient patch of forest was a Shembe church gathering, people in white robes settled in a wide circle on the grass. And beyond them in the valley lay Sweetwaters, Georgetown, Plessislaer, the sprawl of Edendale … the tract of land originally demarcated under Shepstone as the Swartkop reserve, and later designated as a piece of KwaZulu. The houses were small and many. Rondavels and rectangular dwellings, mud walls or concrete blocks, few trees, sparse fields, meandering paths, some new roads.

'It's all owned by the local chief, Inkosi Nsikayezwe Zondi,' Francois said. 'No private titles. Succession tends to be patrilineal, though, which makes it difficult for women when a husband dies and his wife is left without land. AIDS orphans too. They lose their parents, and sometimes they lose their home as well.'

He spoke about the generations vanishing before their stories can be told, and why it is crucial to record oral histories.

We ate our apples and shared a small bar of chocolate. The sun was warm. Blue-and-red speckled butterflies danced across our picnic. A tiny green beetle settled on my hand.

On our left, the regiments of eucalyptus monoculture where nothing else will grow led down to the big tree-filled properties of Blackridge, the abandoned railway line, and the little church. Beyond on that side were Albert Falls, Northdale, World's View. The gravel path back to my mother's house descended through wild grassland that must have been there always.

'That's where the land claim took place,' Francois said, pointing to an open area very close to her end of Uplands Road. 'Albany Road area. It was given to the Botanical Society long ago. But people say they've always been grazing their cattle there, and so they see it as their land.'

Francois seemed more inclined to consider arguments about the legal status of the territory than to ponder the ethics of occupation and dispossession. As for the propertied Blackridge residents, their burglar alarms and big dogs signalled the fear of crime and of poor people.

'It sounds complex,' I said.

'Yes. There are now plans to develop the land, partly to stop another wave of squatters. But the question is what sort of development it's going to be.'

A big eagle flew over.

'Jackal Buzzard,' said Francois. 'There's a saying that when you spot the Yellow-Billed Kite, spring is near. I heard the other day that one has been sighted. They migrate and come back with the spring.'

We walked back down the hill to Blackridge. Instead of taking the path, I made my way through the veld. It was black from burning, and I wanted to feel again the crunch of burnt grass underfoot. It was something my mother knew well, and had taught me to love. Walking down from the Ridge, my body remembered it clearly: the crunch of black stumps beneath your boot, and the bright flare of the green shoots growing back.

9.

That afternoon, I returned to the vanished house at the back of Ian's garden.

'You take your time,' he said when I appeared. 'Just be there. Do what you need to do.'

'Could I pick a lemon?'

'Really,' he said, 'you can pick the whole tree.'

I sat and walked. Wandered on hidden paths. Picked a bag of lemons to take home for marmalade. The fox terrier and the Rottweilers followed me everywhere, gazing soulfully into my eyes. Ian went out and bought a chainsaw for the bugweed and a carrot cake for tea. Michelle helped dig up a clump of snowdrops to plant in our garden in Cape Town.

Afterwards, I sat in the hired car in Uplands Road, holding a copy of the drawing that George Holgate had made in 1884. When a place becomes a map of coloured lines and numbers, however beautifully drawn, we know it has very little to do with the territory. But sometimes, if you're lucky, the map can bring you back.

It was dusk again, and I felt the old loneliness. Next day, I'd be leaving for Cape Town.

A movement in one of the high trees in Natalie's garden caught my attention. Monkeys! The trees and the telephone wires were alive with a troupe of grey vervets. They were scratching, eating, chattering, playing, grooming, hugging their babies, leaping wide from one tree to the next. A young one lay outstretched on a branch, utterly relaxed, while another checked the fur for fleas. Two adolescents chased and snarled. A mother leapt across the sky with her baby clinging on underneath.

Monkey children. Monkey elders. Family. Vermin. They really do know how to play. My mother could have watched them forever.

10.

The big trucks roared down the N3 carrying horses in transit, battery chickens, edible oil, flammable gas, a pile of straight gum poles stripped and ready, and a load of sheep stacked in two storeys, a hundred or more, meek faces gazing through the bars.

It was late spring the following year, and I was driving from King Shaka International Airport to Pietermaritzburg to attend Colin Gardner's funeral. He had died suddenly, and I felt bereft. By the time I reached the church it was raining hard.

'He must have been a great man,' someone said to Mary. 'Look, even Heaven is crying.'

My friend Mike Lambert pulled me into the makeshift choir to sing, Mary gave a brave and beautiful speech, and the old Irish priest spoke of poetry. He said that in Colin the vein of poetry flowed especially strongly. A living stream.

Early the next morning I woke to hear the rainbird calling. A fine mist of rain was falling on leaf and branch, and the house where I was staying rested quietly in a forest of great trees. My feet walked barefoot along stone paths deep in moss and fern. And then I heard it again. *uFukwe*, beloved portent of rain. I'd made no plans to visit Blackridge, and there was not much time before my flight home. But the sound was enough to draw me back. Perhaps her stream had begun to flow.

I parked the car beside the culvert at the bottom of Phindile's garden where I first met the fox terrier. The previous summer, she had sent me pictures of the water running in full spate across her land. Now I bent down to the streambed to look. The earth was damp, but there was no stream. After all, the rains had only just started.

The rainbird called again and the dogs started barking. While the fox terrier looked on attentively, Ian's big Rottweilers rushed at the fence, hurling themselves towards me again and again with open jaws and big teeth, barking and barking with a terrifying intensity. I'd hoped for a quick visit to the garden at the back but that decided it. It was just too frightening. I turned away.

But as I continued to walk to the car, the dogs simply would not stop barking and bounding, and they were so furiously insistent that something made me stop and look at them.

As I did so, I realised that the younger Rottweiler was stretching over the gate towards me not to bite but to greet. Cautiously, I took a step in her direction and she began to whine. I reached out my hand, and she would not stop licking it. What was this if not an invitation? I took a deep breath, unwound the chain from the gate, and stepped into the garden. They nearly knocked me over with joy, escorting me to the door.

'Hello,' Michelle said.

I started making some explanation, but it was unnecessary. She knew who I was.

The dogs and I walked up the broken paths to where the house once stood, and at the far end of the garden we found it. Overgrown with elephant ears, wild ginger, and black-eyed Susan, a little vein of water had begun to flow.

The day was misty. *uFukwe* and the dogs filled the garden with sound. But when they were quiet I could hear it: the voice of the stream.

I said my goodbyes then, and left the garden. Left the city, joined the freight trucks on the highway to Durban, and caught the plane to Cape Town.

This time, I returned empty-handed.

References

Bickham, Troy. 2008. 'Eating the Empire: Intersections of Food, Cookery and Imperialism in Eighteenth-Century Britain'. *Past & Present* 198: 71–109.

Birkett, Frances. 1900. 'Report on Dundee After Boer Occupation.' Unpublished, 27 June 1900.

Bolte Taylor, Jill. 2009. *My Stroke of Insight: A Brain Scientist's Personal Journey.* New York: Penguin Group.

Chidester, David. 2014. *Empire of Religion: Imperialism and Comparative Religion.* Chicago and London: University of Chicago Press.

Cope, Frances. 1883? Untitled manuscript [*Koppie's Story*]. Unpublished.

DeBaggio, Thomas. 2003. *Losing My Mind: An Intimate Look at Life with Alzheimer's.* New York: Free Press.

DeBaggio, Thomas. 2007. *When it Gets Dark: An Enlightened Reflection on Life with Alzheimer's.* New York: Free Press.

Duckitt, Hildagonda. (1891) 1902. *Hilda's "Where Is It?" Of Recipes: Containing Amongst Other Practical And Tried Recipes Many Old Cape, Indian, And Malay Dishes And Preserves: Directions for Polishing Furniture, Cleaning Silk, etc, And A Collection of Home Remedies in Case of Sickness.* London: Chapman & Hall.

Edgecombe, Ruth & Bill Guest. 1986. 'Labour Conditions on the Natal Collieries: The Case of the Dundee Coal Company 1908–1955.' University of the Witwatersrand, African Studies Institute, Seminar Paper, May 1986.

Frawley, Jodi. 2008. 'Making Mangoes Move'. *Transforming Cultures eJournal* 3(1): February 2008.

Guest, Bill. 1989. 'The new economy.' In Andrew Duminy & Bill Guest (eds). *Natal and Zululand from Earliest Times to 1910: A New History.* Pietermaritzburg: University of Natal Press, pp. 302–323.

Guy, Jeff. (1979) 1994. *The Destruction of the Zulu Kingdom.* Pietermaritzburg: University of Natal Press.

Guy, Jeff. 1983. *The Heretic: A Study of the Life of John William Colenso 1814–1883.* Pietermaritzburg: University of Natal Press.

Guy, Jeff. 2001. *The View Across the River: Harriette Colenso and the Zulu Struggle against Imperialism.* Cape Town: David Philip.

Guy, Jeff. 2006. *Remembering the Rebellion: The Zulu Uprising of 1906.* Durban: University of KwaZulu-Natal Press.

Haddad, Beverley. 2016. 'Church Uniforms as an Indigenous Form of Anglicanism: A South African Case Study'. *Journal of Anglican Studies* 14 (2): 156–171.

Hamilton, Carolyn & Leibhammer, Nessa. 2014. 'Salutes, labels and other archival artefacts'. In Carolyn Hamilton & Pippa Skotnes (eds). *Uncertain Curature: In and Out of the Archive*. Cape Town: Jacana, pp. 155–187.

Hamilton, Carolyn & Leibhammer, Nessa. 2016. 'Ethnologised pasts and their archival futures: Construing the archive of southern KwaZulu-Natal pertinent to the period before 1910'. In Carolyn Hamilton and Nessa Leibhammer (eds). *Tribing and Untribing the Archive*, Volume 2. Pietermaritzburg: UKZN Press, pp. 415–449.

Henderson, Sheila. 1982. 'Colonial Coalopolis: The Establishment and Growth of Dundee.' *Natalia* 12: 14–26.

Holmes, PM, Richardson, DM, Esler, KJ, Witkowski, ETF & Fourie, S. 2005. 'A decision-making framework for restoring riparian zones degraded by invasive alien plants in South Africa'. *South African Journal of Science* 101: 553–564.

Ingold, Tim. 2007. *Lines: A Brief History*. London: Routledge.

Kirshner, Howard S. 2004. 'Approaches to Intellectual and Memory Impairments'. In Walter George Bradley (ed.). *Neurology in Clinical Practice: Principles of Diagnosis and Management, Volume 1*. Philadelphia, PA: Butterworth Heinemann, pp. 65–74.

Knackfuss, Hermann. 1899. *Rembrandt*. London: H. Grevel & Co.

Koopman, Adrian & Deane, John. 2005. 'New names for old: Transformation in the streets of Pietermaritzburg'. *Natalia* 35: 85–90.

Lambert, John. 1989. 'From independence to rebellion: African society in crisis, c. 1880-1910'. In Andrew Duminy & Bill Guest (eds). *Natal and Zululand from Earliest Times to 1910: A New History*. Pietermaritzburg: University of Natal Press, pp. 373–401.

Marks, Shula. 1970. *Reluctant Rebellion: The 1906–1908 Disturbances in Natal*. Oxford: Clarendon Press.

Martens, Mary. 1911. *A Woman of Small Account: A South African Social Picture*. London, Felling-on-Tyne, New York, Melbourne: The Walter Scott Publishing Co.

Martin, Arthur Clive. 1969. *The Durban Light Infantry Volume II 1935-1960*. Durban: Hayne & Gibson Limited.

Martin, Michael Clive. 1943. 'Voice of the Libyan Desert'. In Keidrych Rhys (ed.). *More Poems from the Forces: A Collection of Verses by Serving Members of the Navy, Army, and Air Force*. London: George Routledge & Sons, pp. 188–189.

McLelland, R. 1960. *The Pietermaritzburg Technical College 1910–1960*. Pietermaritzburg: City Printing Works, p. 43.

Nasson, Bill. 2010. *The War for South Africa: The Anglo-Boer War 1899–1902*. Cape Town: Tafelberg.

Sandwith, Margaret. 2002. *The diminution of the Mist Belt grasslands of KwaZulu-Natal: An historical investigation of land-use change*. Unpublished dissertation, University of Natal.

Smallie, Alan Watson. c. 1935. *Letters from the Front during the Boer War, 1899–1902, by a member of the Natal Volunteer Force*. Unpublished.

Smallie, Alan Watson. c. 1935. 'Curriculum Vitae'. Untitled, unpublished, unpaginated.

Smallie, Alan Watson. 1902. Uncollected Letters. Unbound.

Smallie, Alan Watson. 1897. *Diary of the Trip of the Natal Volunteers to England for the Festivities at the Diamond Jubilee, 1897*. Unpublished.

Smallie, Elizabeth Madeline. 1952. 'Champagne 7-1-1952'. *Ramblers Journal* February 1952: 10–11.

Smallie, Madeline et al. 1912 – present. Recipes. Unpublished family recipe collection.

Solnit, Rebecca. 2014. *Encylopedia of Trouble and Spaciousness*. San Antonio: Trinity University Press.

Snyder, Gary. 1992. *No Nature: New and Selected Poems*. New York & San Francisco: Pantheon Books.

Tatlow, AH (ed.). 1911. *Natal Province: Descriptive Guide and Official Hand-Book*. Durban: South African Railways Printing Works.

Van der Watt, Lize-Marié. 2010. "'To Kill the Locusts, But Not Destroy the Farmers": Officials, Farmers and the Plagues of the Pharaoh, c. 1920-1935'. *South African Historical Journal* 62(2): 356–383.

Van Sittert, Lance. 2003. 'Our irrepressible fellow colonist: The biological invasion of prickly pear (*Opuntia ficus-indica*) in the Eastern Cape, c.1890–c.1910'. In Stephen Dovers, Ruth Edgecombe and Bill Guest (eds). *South Africa's Environmental History: Cases and Comparisons*. Athens, OH and Cape Town: Ohio University Press and David Philip, pp. 139–159.

Walker, Cherryl. 1990. 'The women's suffrage movement: The politics of gender, race and class'. In Cherryl Walker (ed.). *Women and Gender in Southern Africa to 1945*. Cape Town: David Philip, pp. 313–345.

Watt, Steve. 1999. *The Siege of Ladysmith*. Johannesburg: Ravan Press.

Weyer, Vanessa. 2000. 'Land Transformation in the Karkloof Catchment Between 1944 and 1999: Towards a Database for Future Planning'. Unpublished dissertation, University of KwaZulu-Natal.

Williams, Oscar, (ed.). 1945. *The War Poets: An Anthology of the War Poetry of the 20th Century*. New York: John Day.

Witt, Harald. 2003. 'The Emergence of Privately Grown Industrial Tree Plantations'. In Stephen Dovers, Ruth Edgecombe & Bill Guest (eds). *South Africa's Environmental History: Cases & Comparisons*. Athens, OH and Cape Town: Ohio University Press and David Philip, pp. 90–111.

Thanks

The subject of this book began with my mother, Elizabeth Martin, and its act of love and mourning has become a kind of homage to her extraordinary spirit.

From the very beginning, her grandchildren Sophie and Sky Cope were intimately involved in the project, and their insight and compassion have continued to be a true support. *The Blackridge House* is written for them, and for the other children.

So many sentient beings have contributed to the process, but the following people in particular have my heartfelt gratitude: Francois Marais, my guide through the labyrinth; John Wright, who patiently gave me books to read and whose incisive conversations helped me think about history; Colin Gardner, Mary Gardner, Andrew Naicker, and Joseph Shabalala, for their generous guidance at key moments in the quest; my special guides to the Blackridge garden who appeared in the persons of Kelsey Bartman, Katie Blackmore, Natalie Blackmore, Ian de Villiers, Michelle de Villiers, Lyndy Mansfield, Phindile Shange, and Graham Tegg; Steve Allen, who helped me imagine what it was that I was looking for; Barry Lopez, whose conversations about writing gave me the courage to continue; Gary Snyder, for the interpenetration of house and wild; Heiko Bron, for his helpful networking without which I'd never have found the house; Faeeza Ballim, Cairie Bartman, Andy Blackmore, Rob Burgess, Ken Castelyn, Betty Combrink, Jenny Coetzee, Susan Fantasia, Bridget Harrison, Terry Higginson, Pat Horswell, Eugene Joubert, Aileen Metherell, Willie Schoeman, Dr Silinga, Audrey Tanner, and the other members of the community of Blackridge neighbours whose kind attention to my quest helped to keep it alive; Chris Ballantine, Bill Bizley, Sazi Dlamini, Beverley Haddad, Wally Menne, Nero Moodley, Abner Nyamende, Michelle Rogers, Nkosinathi Sithole, Ian Smallie, Shelagh Spenser, Gill Tatham, Lawrence Tucker, Lance van Sittert, Gavin Whitelaw, and Rose Williams, for specific and crucial assistance with research; Andrew Bank, Steve Cornell, Mark Gevisser, Antjie Krog, Barbara McCrea, Kay McCormick, Kobus Moolman, Nigel Penn, Stan Ridge, and Michael Wessels, for generously reading and commenting on parts of the manuscript, sometimes all of it; Duncan Brown for his ongoing enthusiasm for the project; my colleagues in the English Department at the University of the Western Cape who did my teaching when I needed leave; Nèlleke de Jager, Russell Martin, Na'eemah Masoet, and Meg van der Merwe for their encouragement; Tim Ingold, Gary Snyder, and Rebecca Solnit, for permission to quote from their work; and the staff at Jonathan Ball, especially my publisher Jeremy Boraine and my editor Angela Voges, for the remarkable care they have brought to making the book possible.

I am grateful to the University of the Western Cape and the National Research Foundation for their financial support of this research.

And finally, as always, I'm grateful to Michael Cope for his unfailing companionship along the way, at every level.

Notes

1   In 2009, the second draft of the Alien and Invasive Species Regulations of the National Environmental Management: Biodiversity Act, 2004 (Act No. 10 of 2004) listed *Melia azedarach* under Category 3: invasive species, which require a permit. No permits for these are granted in riparian areas. For a discussion of the local impact of invasive aliens in riparian zones, and a review of procedures to combat this, see PM Holmes et al. (2005).

2   Jodi Frawley gives a useful account of the story of how mangoes tracked through the colonies in J Frawley (2008), pp. 165–184.

3   AW Smallie's unpublished *Diary of the Trip of the Natal Volunteers to England for the Festivities at the Diamond Jubilee, 1897* is the source for this and all subsequent references to the journal.

4   The technical term for this is 'myelination'. As I understand it, when you repeat an activity successively (whether it is playing a particular scale on the piano, doing a cartwheel, or remembering an episode involving a beloved pet), the neural pathway involved becomes stronger as the axon is coated with myelin, or myelinated. In this way we learn how to do things, remember things, etc.

5   In 'Approaches to Intellectual and Memory Impairments' (2004), Howard S Kirshner describes 'remote memory' which seems to resist 'the effects of medial temporal damage; once memory is well stored, probably in the neocortex, it can be retrieved without use of the hippocampal system' (p. 68). He notes too that research indicates that 'overlearned memories gradually become less dependent on the hippocampus' (p. 70).

6   DeBaggio mentions this in *When It Gets Dark: An Enlightened Reflection on Life with Alzheimer's* (p. 201), the second of two extraordinary books. 'After forty years of pussyfooting with words, I finally had a story of hell to tell,' he writes on the opening page of the first book about the experience, *Losing My Mind: An Intimate Look at Life with Alzheimer's* (p. 1). Like my mother, like all of us, he is frightened. Of his condition, and the practice by which he is documenting it, he says later in the same book, 'I am here to mourn memory' (p. 117).

7   The letters comprise two unpublished, undated volumes collected by AW Smallie under the title *Letters from the Front during the Boer War, 1899–1902, by a member of the Natal Volunteer Force.*

8   *Letters from the Front,* p. 131.

9   In *The War for South Africa: The Anglo-Boer War 1899–1902,* Bill Nasson comments that '[l]iberal moral revulsion over the camp policy and condemnation of Britain's perceived perversion of the rules of civilised warfare came to form the most single-

minded political issue of the war' (p. 245). Nasson's subtle and informative history has been my main source for interpreting the events of this period.

10 *Letters from the Front*, p. 62.

11 *Letters from the Front*, p. 61. Nasson remarks on the atrocious state of the hospital camp in Ladysmith during the Siege (p. 166), and notes that during the war British troops 'were far more likely to succumb to a faecal-oral disease borne by water, dust or flies than to a Mauser bullet' (p. 247).

12 *Letters from the Front*, p. 88.

13 *Letters from the Front*, p. 245.

14 *Letters from the Front*, p. 146.

15 *Letters from the Front*, pp. 50–51.

16 AW Smallie *Uncollected Letters*, 11 May 1902.

17 AW Smallie's *Curriculum Vitae* is the source for this and subsequent references to the brief narrative account of his life.

18 See Jeff Guy's *Remembering the Rebellion: The Zulu Uprising of 1906*, which includes a large number of evocative photographs (of forests, hills, settlements, and people), and Shula Marks, *Reluctant Rebellion: The 1906–1908 Disturbances in Natal*.

19 I was intrigued to find in his brief account of this period a note regarding his determination to resign from the Regiment shortly before the Rebellion owing to what he calls excessive unpleasantness and opposition. According to my mother, her father had never had much patience with people in positions of authority whom he considered to be fools and there seem to have been a number of them in the army. This time he appears to have quarrelled with the colonel – who did not accept his resignation until some time later, after he had repeatedly submitted it.

20 *Curriculum Vitae*, n.p.

21 Quoted in R McLelland (1960), p. 43.

22 *Curriculum Vitae*, n.p.

23 *Curriculum Vitae*, n.p.

24 The same product was earlier imported in massive quantities from London for the elimination of another officially designated pest, the prickly pear. On the cultural and ideological values involved in responses to biological invasions by members of the 'invaded society', see Lance van Sittert (2003). For an environmental history of responses to locust invasions in the early twentieth century in South Africa, see Lize-Marié Van der Watt (2010).

25 *Natal Advertiser*, 13 October 1936.

26 *Curriculum Vitae*, n.p.

27 *Koppie's Story*, pp. 9–10.

28 Jeff Guy's biography of Bishop Colenso, *The Heretic*, gives a meticulous and compelling account of the events of these years. In particular, as regards the 'Zulu threat', he shows the extent to which colonial public opinion was manipulated to nurture the idea of this terror (pp. 249–270). See also his *The Destruction of the Zulu Kingdom* (1979, 1994) on the specific strategies involved in the invasion of Zululand.

29 *Koppie's Story*, p. 13.

30 On the position of chiefs such as Inkosi Phakade with regard to the Shepstone administration, see John Lambert (1989, p. 374), and for a discussion of the 'Zulu

war dance' by five hundred men that Phakade convened for Shepstone and other government officials in 1876, as described by Rider Haggard (the first thing he ever wrote for publication), see David Chidester (2014), pp. 146–148.

31 *Koppie's Story*, p. 304.

32 On the escalation of industry and agriculture, the related expansion of communications infrastructure, and an associated accumulation of capital in Natal during the last two decades of the nineteenth century, see Bill Guest, 'The new economy' (1989).

33 The whipoorwill is a North American nightjar, but this is what my mother called the Red-chested Cuckoo, probably because the three-syllable name echoes the structure of its call.

34 *Koppie's Story*, p. 274.

35 Two theses consider the impact of commercial plantations on the Mistbelt grassland ecologies of KwaZulu-Natal. See Vanessa Weyer (2000) and Margaret Sandwith (2002). For a broader environmental history of industrial tree plantations in the region, see publications by Harald Witt, including 'The Emergence of Privately Grown Industrial Tree Plantations' (2003), pp. 90–111.

36 Frances Birkett (1900).

37 This description of the Tatham house is from Sheila Henderson's article 'Colonial Coalopolis: The Establishment and Growth of Dundee', which gives an evocative picture of the economic boom in Dundee in the first decade of the century, and mentions this mansion in particular as being one of those built by an affluent 'crème de la crème' (1982, p. 24).

38 The shocking labour conditions on the Dundee mine are incisively discussed in a paper by Ruth Edgecombe and Bill Guest (1986).

39 See the discussion of this in Troy Bickham's 'Eating the Empire' (2008, p. 103), a compelling analysis of the centrality of food and eating to the British imperial experience during the eighteenth century.

40 This is the figure he gives in the brief narrative account of his civilian life.

41 For more on the *manyano* movement in the Vulindlela area, and a fascinating reflection on the role of women's church uniforms in this context, see Beverley Haddad's 'Church Uniforms as an Indigenous Form of Anglicanism: A South African Case Study' (2016), pp. 156–171.

42 For an analysis of early local expressions of the movement for women's suffrage, see Cherryl Walker (1990).

43 Martens, p. 21.

44 Martens, p. 286

45 Martens, p. 313.

46 'Voice of the Libyan Desert' appeared along with two others in Keidrych Rhys (ed.), *More Poems from the Forces: A Collection of Verses by Serving Members of the Navy, Army, and Air Force*, pp. 188-189. See also his entries in Oscar Williams (ed.), *The War Poets: An Anthology of War Poetry of the Twentieth Century* (1945).

47 Messages to the troops on the eve of the battle from Lieutenant-General Montgomery and Major-General Pienaar are quoted in my grandfather Arthur Clive Martin's regimental history, *The Durban Light Infantry* Volume II 1935–1960 (1969), p. 283.

48   View this image at http://campbell.ukzn.ac.za/?q=node&page=360.

49   AH Tatlow (ed.) (1911), p. 147.

50   The uncertain siting of the kraal is discussed in some detail in Peter Alcock's wide-ranging 'histo-geographical' essay of place, 'The Hills Above Pietermaritzburg: An Appreciation', available at https://www.duct.org.za/education/23-hills-above-pietermaritzburg.html.

51   This account of the British Association's visit derives from two fascinating recent articles. See Carolyn Hamilton and Nessa Leibhammer (2014), and Carolyn Hamilton and Nessa Leibhammer (2016). The key insight here is to read the entire collection (both the artefacts brought back from Swartkop *and* the colonial artefacts and strategies of collection and classification by which the materials from 'Laduma's Kraal' were assembled and interpreted) as an archive.

52   Thanks too, to Nkosinathi Sithole for a subsequent conversation about the translation. He pointed out that the song is being sung by a woman to her suitor rather than her lover.

53   EM Smallie, p. 10.

54   EM Smallie, p. 11.

55   For an informative discussion of the new street names, see Adrian Koopman and John Deane (2005).

56   The spelling of this name has proved difficult to verify. Aside from this reference to the title deed, I have chosen to follow the spelling used on long-time Blackridge neighbour John Tanner's map, which has it as 'Nicol'. As John's wife, Audrey Tanner, explained it to me, there were two families who lived at Blackridge: Nicol and Nicholls.

57   This question refers to the evocative work of Tim Ingold in *Lines: A Brief History*, specifically his discussion of 'lines of occupation' and his acknowledgement of novelist Georges Perec's comment that these are lines 'for which millions of people have died' (p. 85).

58   Steve Watt (1999), p. 3.

59   I'm grateful to John Wright for emphasising, in conversation, the aspects of settler mentality that appear to have derived from their relative poverty in Britain, and what he called their 'desperate pursuit of gentility as laid down back home'.